An Evolutionary
View of
Economic Growth

AN EVOLUTIONARY VIEW OF ECONOMIC GROWTH

ASHOK S. GUHA

CLARENDON PRESS · OXFORD
1981

Oxford University Press, Walton Street, Oxford OX2 6DP

London Glasgow New York Toronto
Delhi Bombay Calcutta Madras Karachi
Kuala Lumpur Singapore Hong Kong Tokyo
Nairobi Dar es Salaam Cape Town
Melbourne Auckland
and associate companies in
Beirut Berlin Ibadan Mexico City

Published in the United States by
Oxford University Press, New York

British Library Cataloguing in Publication Data
Guha, Ashok S.
An evolutionary view of economic growth.
1. Economic development
I. Title
339.5   HB199
ISBN 0-19-828431-4

Typeset by Oxprint Ltd, Oxford
and Printed in Great Britain
at the University Press, Oxford
by Eric Buckley
Printer to the University

To
Indrani
and
Ahana

PREFACE

THE plight of a pure theorist confronted suddenly by the real world is always amusing and often pathetic. Such was my predicament when—as a fledgling economic theorist of the purest variety—I found myself trying to understand and teach the hard facts of development history. Out of this hilarious situation came the present work.

My ideas as they developed were deeply influenced by contacts with colleagues and students at the School of International Studies, Jawaharlal Nehru University. These belonged to a whole spectrum of different disciplines—economists, political scientists, historians, sociologists, psychologists, and geographers. It is a unique feature of the school that it provides a focus for the convergence of such a cluster of diverse interests.

This book was very long in gestation. The friend who—looking at the slimness of the volume—had much to say about the elephant in labour which begat a mouse could not have been more justified. A crucial phase of the gestation period, however, was the time I spent at the Institute of Development Studies, Sussex in 1974. Here I enjoyed both the leisure and the stimulus that I needed to develop and clarify my ideas. I am deeply grateful to the Institute for providing me this opportunity.

Thanks are also due to the Reserve Bank of India which supplied unquestioningly the research and travel funds I occasionally needed for my work.

On the personal level my profoundest debt is to John Hicks for the unfailing interest and constant encouragement which sustained me in seeing this book through to publication. I am also deeply indebted to Amartya Sen who—despite his usual frantic schedule—never failed to spare the time and interest I demanded of him. I have benefited greatly from the comments and suggestions of many others. Particular mention should, however, be made of Kaushik Basu, Sabyasachi Bhattacharya, Kenneth Binmore, Sukhamoy Chakravarti, A. K. Das Gupta, Partha Das Gupta, Mrinal Dutta Choudhury, Mark Elvin, Sanjay Lall, S. P. Nag, and Ashvani Saith. I must also thank my graduate students whose endless questioning spurred me to develop the ideas presented here. Finally, a special word of thanks is due to my colleague Alokesh Barua for the enormous pains he took over the editing and preparation of this manuscript.

ASHOK GUHA

CONTENTS

Part One

1

INTRODUCTION

THE test of any scientific hypothesis is its ability to explain observed phenomena. By this token, the most important test of economics as a science lies surely in explaining why rapid economic growth occurs in particular places at particular times. Yet economic theory has had precious little to say about this. Our growth men have amused themselves with growth models galore, but these growth processes are determined by a range of parameters and initial conditions; they would trace the chequered temporal and spatial pattern of growth to temporal and spatial differences in these parameters and initial conditions, but do nothing at all to account for these differences. An economy might grow because its savings function or its production function or its innovation possibility function has shifted, or perhaps because it has just received a big enough push from its government. But the causes of these shifts lie outside the pale of economics. They may be due to a chance discovery or a ruler's caprice, to the Protestant ethic or to toilet-training practices—we don't know what, and we don't really care.

In thus surrendering to the sociologist or the political scientist the job of explaining the timing and locale of economic growth, economics has taken a great leap backwards from science towards theology. Abandon the search for an economic explanation of observed economic growth, and economics becomes largely an exercise in irrelevance, a scholastic game of logic-chopping and puzzle-solving.

It is evident, however, that any meaningful analysis of the development process requires an exploration of the delicate tracery of relationships between the economic, political, and social variables in society. In treading this maze one needs a guiding thread, a principle to direct one's steps; and the classic example of an approach unified by such a directive principle is the Marxian. Marx sought the key to social processes in the ultimately determining role of economic factors, and specifically in class relations and their interaction with technology. Marxian tradition shows how a beautifully complete picture of social change can be developed on this basis. In this sense all subsequent thinkers who have sought some kind of a total view of society are profoundly indebted to Marx.

There are, however, two well-known problems that beset the Marxian approach. The first may be described as the fallacy of first causes. In assigning to economic factors an ultimately determining value—however remote—in human affairs, one necessarily subscribes to the primacy of economic necessity over man's other needs. One must eat—it may be argued—before one can think of anything else. But to put it thus is to realize how limited a picture this is of the imperatives of human survival; for men must not only eat, but also defend their lives against enemies; and—in any continuing society—they must also reproduce. Protection and procreation are just as basic to human existence as production. Indeed, I hope in this book to show that in many societies it is the security problem and the military organization of society which is of central importance. It need hardly be added that the organization of society dictated by security needs may be very different from that required by maximal production.

Secondly, even if one concedes—for argument's sake—the primacy of economic considerations, one may doubt the class interpretation of economic motives. Do men behave primarily as members of a class, or as individuals in complex and multi-faceted roles? Are the common interests of the members of a Marxian class strong enough to transcend the conflicts between them and their cross-links with individuals of other classes? To give a specific example, the Marxian analysis of the Meiji Revolution runs essentially in terms of an alliance between the feudal warrior class (the *samurai*) and a very much subordinate mercantile interest. Yet the first decade of Meiji saw not only a decisive repudiation of feudal institutions but also a planned and progressive impoverishment of the *samurai* so extreme as to drive them to the Satsuma Rebellion, the most formidable threat that the Meiji regime was to face. A class analysis of the resolutely anti-feudal behaviour of the Meiji government requires all manner of intellectual contortions. An infinitely simpler—and therefore aesthetically superior—explanation would visualize the Meiji oligarchy not primarily as representatives of the *samurai,* but as a group of men who were driven by the compulsions of power into a set of policies which did not really reflect their class origins and loyalties. This requires, of course, an analysis of the logic of power which may in these circumstances be more compelling than that of class.

It may no doubt be argued that exactitude in explanation is an impossible dream in the social sciences, that approximations are all one may ask for, and that the class interpretation of social change is as good an approximation to reality as any. But the scientific approach also implies that we investigate every discrepancy between model and reality and never abandon the search for a closer approximation.

Further, one may question whether the class model is all that good a frame of reference for social reality. A class is a group of individuals with essentially similar roles in the productive process. In any complex society with a highly developed division of functions among its members and associated specialized skills, no class can function well in isolation. Each requires the co-operation of complementary groups. A class therefore lacks cohesiveness, bargaining power, and the ability to withstand conflict. The effective entities in any situation of social conflict are not classes but coalitions across classes. This is not to deny that a given class may outlive its productive role in the social process and be squeezed out by a combination of other classes. Indeed, the extinction of the rentier— by which we mean those who are not engaged in current efforts for production, defence, or any other essential social function—is a phenomenon we shall repeatedly invoke. But this, of course, is not all there is to the class analysis of social history.

A second approach to social change along the lines we visualize is represented by Hicks's classic *Theory of Economic History*(27). Unfortunately, Hicks limits himself to a model of the evolution of the market economy with its political and legal corollaries through all its phases. He does not concern himself with the obverse problem—the growth of the command economy. He analyses the political correlates of the rise of the market, but ignores the imperatives of military security. The picture that emerges is not comprehensive or complete, though suggestive enough to be the principal inspiration for the present work. It is a picture that derives its unity from a common theme rather than from a common principle *à la* Marx.

In this book, I follow the Marxian method of looking for a unifying thread in a postulate about human nature and not the Hicksian method of focusing on a central theme. But I reject the

Marxian postulate of the primacy of economic motivation and concentrate instead on the essential biological laws that rule the entire living world. The unifying principle in human behaviour thus lies in the imperatives of survival; but these, as mentioned earlier, extend well beyond considerations of mere sustenance. Recent work in ethology has highlighted the central role in animal societies of instincts other than the drives for food, shelter, or even sex. In particular, the survival value of the dominance instinct and of aggression (including intra-specific aggression) has been much emphasized. All these are aspects of behaviour which do not derive in any sense from some more basic search for food; they represent parallel instincts with an evolutionary justification and a value of their own. In human societies, the logic of survival is at least as complex; and, while in this book I seek to capture some of this essential and realistic complexity, one cannot but regret losing the elegant simplicity of the Marxian mode.

On the other hand, this book is much too brief for any likeness to the rich tapestry of motives and institutions that is the stuff of history. In particular, it focuses on the environmental changes to which societies adapt. But social change reflects not only environmental pressures but also inherited structure; and, while this point is developed in the theoretical analysis, its empirical illustration (as with China and Japan) is confined to political-military structures only. The emphasis is on the state; and this ignores a whole world of institutions—the family, the kin-group, the caste, the class, the peer-group, the religious community. None of these have the coercive power of the modern state; but all wield some measure of authority over the individual. Also ignored in the case studies are inherited value systems—social ideologies, religious beliefs, personal values. This is not to deny their influence on history, but to focus in specific cases on the smallest possible set of essential explanatory variables. All this makes for bad historiography. That unfortunately is the price one must pay for clarity and economy of exposition.

2

THE ADAPTATION OF HUMAN SOCIETIES TO
THEIR ENVIRONMENT

THE ultimate basis of all behavioural sciences is biology. Opinions may differ on the nature of man in many of its aspects; but the one axiomatic truth about him is that he is a species of life and is subject as such to the general laws of life—the laws of evolution and natural selection. He is, of course, unique among the species; but his gifts of language and rational thought, his large slow-growing brain, his consequent ability to learn from his ancestors and from his own experience and thus to accumulate over generations a fund of knowledge and tradition—while all quite distinctive—do not enable him to transcend the evolutionary process. They reflect in fact its selective pressures. They have developed as weapons of survival, as means of adaptation to the environment; and all the products of man's specific abilities—his culture, his technology, his modes of political, social, and economic organization—cannot be understood except in terms of their adaptive value.

Biological adaptation is both autoplastic and alloplastic: it involves changes in the gene pool of the species as well as manipulation of the environment. We now know that man, through social control of his breeding, has vastly accelerated the tempo of genetic change. Mathematical geneticists like Sewall Wright (68) have established that the fastest rate of genetic change results not from random breeding but from assortative mating within relatively homogeneous groups to develop well-differentiated strains coupled with occasional interbreeding between groups to facilitate new genetic combinations. Such conditions are ensured in human society by social stratification. Marriage and breeding typically conform to social strata—a conformity that becomes increasingly rigid as the society settles into stagnation. Caste systems are the formal embodiment of the genetic principle of inbreeding. But sporadic interbreeding always persists—through social mobility, internal upheaval, or alien intrusion. Man thereby maintains the optimal conditions for his genetic evolution (Darlington (9)).

Nevertheless, since he is a slow-breeding species, the evolution of his genetic base remains sluggish. His primary mode of adaptation is alloplastic. His technology, his goods, and equipment are all part of this adaptation. Their development over time reflects changes in his relationship to nature, but are focused on the unvarying ends of biological evolution.

The central theme of this book arises out of these considerations. It is that economic growth is best interpreted as an extension of the evolutionary process. This does not mean a resurrection of a social Darwinism of the Spencerian 'survival of the fittest' variety. Nor does it imply the unlinear evolutionism of the *stage theories of growth* in all their variations from Marx to Rostow. All these approaches employ only the *analogy* of organic evolution. They examine society itself as an organism evolving over time—a concept which, despite its similarity to that of the evolving individual organism, has in fact no place whatsoever in biological evolution. This book, on the other hand, visualizes economic growth not merely as analogous to evolution, but as an integral part of it.

Economic growth , of course, must not be viewed in isolation. It is inextricably interwoven with political, social, and cultural change which are all part of the web of evolutionary adaptation. Fortunately, a common thread runs through all this intricacy and lends it unity. For political, social, and cultural phenomena—and economic phenomena too—are not primary but adaptive; and it is necessary at this point to dwell a while on the way in which communities—and the individuals composing them—adapt to their milieu in all the varied but interrelated facets of their behaviour.

The Adaptive Process in Individuals and Societies

A model of cultural adaptation is necessary because the better-known theories of society tend rather to overlook the influence of the environment on the social system. Parsons and his school, for instance, visualize society as a network of institutions which takes on a life of its own: the social system in this view maintains an internal equilibrium which is largely insulated from external circumstances. Others—such as the Marxians—think of society in terms of conflict rather than equilibrium—but conflict nonetheless with its own inner laws of motion, its peculiar dynamics essentially independent of the environment. In disputing these views I do not, of course, deny the compulsions imposed by the structure and inner logic—or dialectic—of a society. However, the essence of my argument is that the social process is not a juggernaut with a self-generated momentum, but an adaptation to the external milieu—lagged and sluggish perhaps, but an adaptation all the same. In order to pursue this point one needs to show how the environment affects individual motivations and how the resulting actions of individuals may either perpetuate or transform the social structure.

Natural selection has endowed the individual organism with an instinctual apparatus for survival comprising at least the self-preservative and sexual instincts. This is the minimum instinctual heritage of all living things. These instincts guide the individual in interacting with and manipulating the physical and social environment to which he is exposed right from birth. Survival is an exercise in adapting to this milieu. Adaptation, however, is not just a matter of a consciously calculated response to the stresses of the present but also the formation of habits, of automatic behaviour patterns which tend to outlive the circumstances of their origin. Habitual unconscious reflexes are a particularly important adaptive mode in infancy—when the individual's repertoire of manipulative abilities and his reasoning powers are limited; hence, one's early life colours and overshadows all one's future behaviour. In general, individual adaptation tends on this account to lag behind environmental change—a lag that sometimes amounts almost to a generation gap. All the same, the individual retains some fraction of his uniquely human capacity to learn throughout his life and can, therefore, cope with change—if only by delayed reaction.

The individual's behaviour spans two distinct domains. First it caters for his strictly physical needs—for food, comfort, sexual opportunity. Second, it answers to the needs and satisfactions that link him to others—the desires for recognition and approval, for superiority and power. Both sets of needs are imperative for survival—the first for obvious reasons, the second because it is instrumental in maintaining the co-operative structures that men need to achieve their physical ends.

The basic evolutionary unit, however, is not the individual but the society to which he relates, a cultural community which in man is the focus of the adaptive process. I visualize the members of society at any moment as participants in a game in which the strategic options include withdrawal from society (with the costs of any conflict that may result taken into account in the pay-offs). The individual's choice of strategy is determined by the pay-off structure of the game. In general, the pay-offs depend not only on the strategies of each individual but also on the environment. The aggregate supply of any good for the members of a society is limited by its productive and exchange opportunities and, therefore, by its natural resources and its external economic milieu. Likewise, victory in battle with its spoils and its accrual in prestige for the warrior is not uniquely determined by the warrior's actions; it depends not only on the performance and strength of the foe, but also on the entire logistic structure supporting the warrior and, therefore, on all the environmental determinants of economic performance. Certain pay-offs, however, are completely institutionalized. Their level depends only on the members of society preserving the institutional structure and is independent of the environment. Thus payments may be contractually guaranteed, rights and obligations underwritten by tradition or constitution, rewards and penalties left to the discretion of established authorities. Whenever individuals co-operate, whether in production, defence, or the maintenance of law and order, a chain of command necessarily evolves—for co-ordination, for the settlement of conflicts or for the coercive enforcement of obligations. Indeed, hierarchies are universal in animal societies and status so overwhelming a preoccupation that dominance is regarded by ethologists as a goal as basic as sex or self-preservation. The authority structure exerts some control over the pattern of rewards and penalties and inevitably insulates some of them from the effects of the environment.

Such is the broad framework of the game of social interaction—its players, strategies, and pay-offs. Now, the continued existence and stability of a society imply, first, that no coalition of its members finds secession a worthwhile strategy, and, secondly, that the social order lies within the core of the game—that no conceivable coalition can improve its lot by departing from the equilibrium set of strategies. If these conditions are not fulfilled, the society would either disintegrate into smaller fragments or transform its internal structure.

The conditions, however, imply that, in any stable society, everyone always deploys such power as he can marshal—individually or in any coalition—to the hilt. Given the pay-off matrix, each individual employs his best strategy (including coalitional strategies); there are no unexhausted reserves of power.

In such a model, social change is the consequence of change in the pay-off matrix. Many elements in this matrix are ecologically determined; they are affected by changes in the relationship of the society to its environment. Such changes, therefore, lead some people to expect pay-offs from social change and to consider forming coalitions to secure it. Those interested in conserving the existing order will have to form counter-coalitions and so bear up with a reduction in their individual pay-offs. Social changes will be effected if the gains they promise to gainers exceed the possible losses of losers . This means either that the gainers can bribe the losers into accepting the change, or that they—and not the losers—can forge the coalitions necessary to impose their objectives on society. Changes in the environment then upset the balance of power within any society and induce a realignment of the social order according to the new power possibilities. Society, in short, adapts to the new ecological parameters.

Some dynamic effects in this equilibrating process—though already touched upon—call for elaboration. First, the adjustment to equilibrium is retarded by the existence of institutionally determined pay-offs which create vested interest in the perpetuation of such institutions. But this is the price of the existence of society itself; and, since man cannot survive without society, it is hardly something that can be described on balance as dysfunctional.

The second of these inertial factors is the force of habit. As already indicated, individual choice —like other aspects of human behaviour—is a matter of learned responses which may initially be adaptive but tend thereafter to become merely habitual. During the total dependence of childhood in particular, the individual is compelled to make drastic adjustments to the prevailing external realities—adjustments which become so deeply embedded in his unconscious, so moulded into his personality as to become almost a part of him. Of course, habit—even when petrified into preference patterns and character structures—is not as immutable as inherited instinct. It is, nevertheless, an influence which leads the individual to undervalue changes in his environment and to seek to conserve his social and physical milieu.

At the other pole from habit is innovation. In my game-theoretic framework, innovation has the effect of revealing strategic options hitherto unknown and changing thereby the pay-off structure of those that are familiar. But the essence of the innovative process lies in the breaking of habits of thought; it involves the transcending of intellectual frames of reference, of interpretations of phenomena, deeply ingrained through education, useful in understanding the known, but a barrier to any awareness of unseen possibilities. Innovation, of course, is so central a part of the adaptive process that it warrants detailed discussion by itself later. For the present, I note that, together with the spread of successful innovations through imitative learning, it constitutes the basic mechanism of social change.

The duality between the mechanisms of stability and those of change within a society is parallel to a similar duality in the domain of genetics. The genes contain within themselves the secret of invariant reproduction, the replication from generation to generation of the same organizing pattern of heritable characteristics. Yet they are subject to mutation at a very small given rate; and, when the environment no longer permits the persistence of the old trait, a highly successful mutant may emerge through selective pressures.

I have discussed, then, the adaptive mechanisms of societies as well as the rigidities implied by the nature of the individual organism and of society itself. The rigidities in the values and power relationships are the fossilized residues of successful adaptation; but in changed circumstances they tend to commit a society to an obsolete way of life. If the adaptive mechanisms are incapable of breaking the mould of tradition, the society itself may disintegrate into smaller, more flexible units; or it may simply die out—through conquest and massacre, starvation or reproductive failure. In the last analysis, natural selection between societies comes into play ensuring the survival only of the successfully adapted.

This picture of society corresponds to the functional-structural view, as seen, for example, by Malinowski (38). Society is visualized as an integrated whole, the structure of which reflects its functions (in our case, essentially the functions that ensure its biological survival). But I reject the Parsonian model of a closed, self-sufficient, stable social system (44). Society, in our view, never composes an equilibrium by itself—but always in conjunction with nature and other societies. Where its relationship with nature is invariant because of mechanisms which stabilize population relative to natural resources, where further it is effectively isolated from other societies—perhaps because of geography—a society may replicate itself generation after generation in an unvarying mould. The stable environment, the social institutions, the sanctions that they jointly determine, the behaviour that is thereby induced must then all be consistent with each other. But the possibility of change—whether due to the internal dynamics of population growth or to exposure to other societies always exists.

A distinctive feature of my model is the stress on the inter-personal character of social processes. The Parsonian concept of the individual, as merely playing a role prescribed for him by social institutions in a grand drama essentially beyond his conscious control, is alien to it. Social institutions in it are nothing but ways in which individuals tend to behave in relation to each other; their existence does not foreclose the variety of strategic options open to the individual, though it does tend to impart a degree of inertia to his choices. In game-theoretic terms, the Parsonian model approximates to the infinite-person game in which there are an infinite number of identical players of each conceivable kind. The individual then has no alternative but to accept social parameters as given. Such a game is a limiting and rather implausible variant of our general model.

In my formulation of the social process, then, social institutions are not immutable facts of life. Neither is the Marxian abstraction of class a central concept. The class—in our analysis—is one kind of coalition. But no individual is ever irrevocably committed to any coalition. He continues in it only in so far as it serves his interests. Of course, the inculcation of class consciousness, like the inculcation of a sense of community within a coalition, may colour his perception of his interests and thereby lend a measure of stability to his class. Yet the effective social groupings in our analysis are not cohesive entities like the Marxian classes, but shifting alliances surviving on the precarious brink of dissolution due to the counter-attraction of other possible coalitional patterns.

Survival Requirements of Human Societies

Such is the process by which men and their cultures adapt to the environment. There are further certain minimum requirements for survival in all cultures. Indeed, the adaptive process comprises the protection of these requirements against the stresses of environmental change. Some of these are the biological imperatives that evolution imposes on the entire animal kingdom. Every animal society—including all human societies as well—requires protection, procreation, and sustenance. The distinctive features of the human life cycle—the prolonged dependence of the child and the import- ance of learning rather than instinct for his survival—add a fourth requirement to this trinity: the necessity of providing for the growth and education of children. Together this quartet of needs rules all human history. It establishes by natural selection the primary func- tions of society—since a society which fails to supply any of these needs adequately cannot survive.

This formulation evokes a question: what does adequate func- tioning imply in each of these fields? I would suggest three aspects of an answer to this question. First, the standards of adequacy for survival are not fixed; they vary with the challenge of the environ- ment. Thus adequacy in procreation implies a higher birth rate in a society exposed to a higher risk of death from external military pressure or on account of an unfavourable natural resource base for production. Secondly, and by the same token, the requirements of adequate fulfilment of one of these needs are closely dependent on social performance in the other fields. To cite the birth rate again: given the external environment, a higher level of military or pro- ductive efficiency reduces the death rate and therefore the fertility requirements for survival. In this sense, efficiency in satisfying one of these needs is a substitute for efficiency in satisfying another. Finally, there is a certain inter-temporal relationship between what a society achieves today and what it must achieve tomorrow in order to survive. This relationship follows from the logic of the human maturation process; a generation nurtured to survive and reproduce in one environment cannot readily adapt to survival in another vastly inferior. Not only does it lack the skills that this requires; but further, its values, its habits, its tastes, even indeed its metabolism and general physiology have been so transformed by its upbringing that its subsistence requirements are altogether higher than if it had been bred to lesser affluence. The implication is that improvements in living standards can be built into the biological system in the short run as subsistence requirements; an over-shooting of the sub- sistence level of the present generation—as may happen in the process of adaptation—becomes irreversible, and any subsequent increase in population may have to be supported at the new higher consumption standard.

Environmental Variables Faced by Societies

The survival requirements represent the objectives that a society must achieve amidst the flux of environmental change. But what are the main variables in the environment?

The first, of course, is the shifting ecological balance between the population of a community and the natural resources which it commands. This includes factors like secular climatic change (invoked by geographers like Huntington (31) to explain many of the major events in history), resource depletion, and—above all— population growth. Indeed, a buoyant population—given the rigidity of subsistence requirements—is a most compelling force for economic development.

Nature, however, is only one of the environmental factors to which a society must adapt. There is also the impact of other societies. On the one hand, there are the predatory pressures of military competition; on the other, the opportunities for enlarging the consumption possibility set through co-operation in production and exchange. These interactions—both the predatory and the co-operative—are such as might be expected between any set of species. But the vast human capacity for learning implies other distinctive kinds of relationship between human communities. It implies in particular the diffusion of knowledge—the flow of learning processes, induced by intensive contact between societies, which transmits new technologies of production, of consumption, of medicine, even indeed of social and political organization.

It is in the perspective of these environmental factors that I seek to view economic growth. I visualize it essentially as an adaptation to four main forces: of population pressure on natural resources, of economic opportunities due to trade and transfer, of military competition, and of demonstration effects. Of course, it cannot be understood without reference to the other dimensions of the adaptive process; and it will be my endeavour to explore some of the essential links between the economic and the non-economic aspects of the total pattern of adaptation.

Consequences of the Evolutionary View of Growth

It remains for me to spell out some of the implications of the evolutionary viewpoint on economic growth.

First, all historical processes which I regard as growth are associated with an improvement in biological indices. Population grows;
life expectancy rises; the onset of puberty is accelerated and the
productive span lengthens; the size and strength of the typical
individual increases. The economist conceives of growth in terms of
increase in *per capita* income. Yet, even if I assume away the
classical perplexities of income measurement—the index number
problem, the imputation problem, the income-distribution
problem, and the like—the logical validity of the *per capita* income
measure itself rests on its interpretation in terms of the welfare of
the typical individual. Such an interpretation is possible only if
utility functions remain invariant over the growth process. But
changes in tastes are an essential part of growth—often indeed its
primary driving force; and in this perspective, the *per capita* income
criterion loses its meaning. Development, then, should be
measured in terms of the simpler phenomena that accompany it;
and, while a variety of trends have been identified as the empirical
correlates of growth, none has been so universally realized as biological improvement. I suggest that this is no accident of history—
that it reflects in fact the natural orientation of evolution.

A second consequence of the evolutionary character of growth is
a certain similarity in rhythm between the two processes. The
evolutionary process has its phases. First, natural selection among
variations establishes a successful adaptation to a particular environment. There follows the rapid expansion of the adapted
species in the new environment up to the limits that the adaptation
allows. New adaptation might set off spurts of renewed growth until
the species is as perfectly attuned to its environment as is genetically
possible for it. It has now reached the outer limits of its growth. It
remains, thereafter, in a stationary equilibrium with its milieu till
this itself changes. The change in environment would evoke new
adaptive responses unless the species has become so rigidly
specialized to the older situation as to be incapable of the new
adjustment.

The rhythm of economic growth is essentially identical. Once an
innovation establishes itself in competition with others as best
suited to an environment, rapid growth ensues. It continues till the
retarding pressure of resource scarcity is felt. Hereafter, a new
phase of adaptive innovation and growth may begin, or—if the
technological leap required by this is too large—a stationary equi-

librium would be maintained. A change in the environment would revive the entire sequence of events and possibilities. It may also, however, raise the spectre of extinction—if the minimum adaptation now necessary for survival is too drastic.

The third implication of the evolutionary model for growth theory arises from absence of parallel or convergent evolution in different isolated environments. The course of evolution in each environment reflects instead its distinctiveness. So does the course of economic growth . Stage theories of growth—which visualize development in terms of uniform sequences of stages in different countries—ignore this diversity of natural environments in which growth occurs, and the diversity of adaptations that it induces. This is true of perfectly isolated as well as of communicating economies. Transport and communication draw different countries into a single global growth process. But they assign them different roles and sequences of development determined by their resource bases. Contact makes for interdependence, not parallel evolution—except in similar milieux.

Finally, the characteristics of biological adaptation hold the key to a better understanding of the innovative process. Structural adaptations of living species almost always follow behavioural changes. A new activity imposed by the environment requires a new use of some organ of the organism. Natural selection then remoulds the organ in the form most efficient for the new activity. There is no unique correspondence between behaviour and organ. Different species may perform the same function using entirely different organs with consequently different structural adaptations; it depends on the prior structure and behaviour of the species—and, even after taking all these into account, the adaptation would retain an essentially random unpredictable aspect, resulting in part from the stochastic nature of the underlying genetic processes.

Innovations have a similar course and character. His environment at a particular time imposes on man certain necessities in terms of goods and activities which induce innovations. But these necessities can be satisfied in different ways—by innovations derived from quite different areas of knowledge and using quite different resources. The environment again exerts its selective pressure in favour of the most efficient way of satisfying needs. Even so, there remains an irreducible aura of blind chance about the precise configuration of an innovation. Indeed if it were not somewhat unpredictable, it would not be an innovation at all. Its long-run consequences, therefore, cannot be foreseen until it actually takes place.

Thus, if I am proposing a deterministic model of development, it is at least a model of statistical rather than rigidly mechanistic determinacy. History can be explained in terms of our evolutionist principles, but it cannot be deduced from them. The actual scenario of development remains unpredictable because it is not a matter of unique necessity but of recurrent chance. Every stage in the sequence follows from the last as one of a set of probabilities rather than a rigidly inevitable consequence. Development is a stochastic process, not a royal road down which the world economy is propelled by some inexorable Newtonian law of motion.

Related to this point is an important methodological issue. My analysis cannot generate refutable predictions, and will not as such satisfy the religious Popperian, for whom predictive content is the distinctive trait of scientific propositions. But the theory of evolution has no predictive power either. Its value is entirely explanatory. So, for that matter—as Popper (49) himself says (censoriously, of course)—is the value of Freudian psychoanalysis. This book, too, is an exercise in explanation only; and, if it has any fruitfulness in this direction, I hope that the reader will forgive my lapses from Popperian orthodoxy.

3

THE POLITICS OF ADAPTATION

WHILE the last chapter dwelt on the sociology of adaptation in its most general sense, the present focuses specifically on the political dimensions of the adaptive process. What, one may ask, is the relevance of all this for the economist? The answer, briefly, is that a model of the political process is indispensable for an analysis of economic development, for it is the structure of authority in any society that sets the rules of the game for its economic units. In particular, it delimits the spheres of the market and command economies and determines the operations of the latter. Thus, it defines the modes of communication and interaction between different participants in the economy. Even *laissez-faire* is an act of policy: it rests on a political decision, first, to provide the minimal infrastructure of law and security that the survival of the market requires, and, secondly, to disengage the state from any further role in the economy. Such acts of policy—whether of active participation or passive withdrawal—are central to the development process; and excluding them and their determinants from our jurisdiction would be the surest way to reduce any attempt at understanding economic growth to an exercise in futility.

In essence, this chapter argues

1. that the state is based on a bargaining equilibrium in a game in which all strategies, including that of force, are open to all its members,
2. that political changes, therefore, are determined by changes in either the preference patterns of the players or the pay-off structure of the game,
3. that given the stabilizing influence of the environment in the formation of tastes, changes in preference patterns would result typically from sudden exposure to alien consumption patterns,
4. that changes in pay-offs from alternative strategies can be accounted for by changes in three main factors: the population/ natural resources balance, the military pressure of surrounding states, and the opportunities for earning from the outside world.

The Contractualist Model of the State

The traditional liberal model of the state is the contractual one. The state, according to a long line of philosophers from Plato through Rousseau to Parsons, is based on a community of interests; it is the purveyor of external economies and public goods which the isolated action of atomistic individuals cannot supply. Voluntary transactions between individuals are based on 'the exclusion principle'—the possibility of excluding one from the services provided by the other; that is the guarantee of appropriate payment for services rendered or cost incurred. But over a wide area of economic life, such exclusion is impossible, consumption is independent of payment and costs of compensations. If things here are left to the volitional interaction of individuals, services essential for all will remain unprovided and costs disastrous for the community at large cannot be controlled. Hence the need for a coercive apparatus within the community. The economic basis of the state then lies in functions like

1. defence and war,
2. law and order,
3. currency,
4. certain kinds of communication,
5. pollution control and civic hygiene,
6. flood control and major irrigation,
7. technical progress,
8. education,
9. the maintenance of full employment,
10. the formation of national monopolies to improve terms of trade with the outside world,
11. planning and policy for economic development.

A word should perhaps be interposed about each of the factors listed above. Defence against predators and collective aggression against prey are the classic primary functions of any biological group—from the troop of baboons to the wolf pack. Law and order—internal security and the peaceful settlement of disputes—are equally basic, being just as indispensable for the group's survival. These two functions indeed sum up the justification for many states. Empires in particular often constitute large areas within which production and trade may multiply in peace. The Pax Romana was indispensable for the growth of the ancient

Mediterranean economy just as Britain's 'Empire of the Sea' made possible the global expansion of ocean trade in the eighteenth and nineteenth centuries. The Chinese Empire's main economic function was security—the provision of a political framework within which the peasant could plough his furrow in peace. Indeed defence today consumes by far the major part of every nation's budget, with police and the judiciary accounting for much of the remainder.

The monetary function is by contrast a recent affair. It dates from the time when monetary needs outstripped the stock of precious metals and gave rise to a need for fiat money. Since fiat money is virtually costless, it offers a large return on the right of seigniorage and the money-maker has a continuous incentive to over-expand money supply. This, in turn, would erode the store-of-value function of money, undermine confidence, and lead in the long run to the collapse of the monetary system. In the long run, however, any given private individual is dead. Only the immortal state can be in principle the source of fiat money.

Road building is, of course, a historic function of the state. The Roman dominions were knit together by their fabled network of roads as was the Inca Empire. The highways of Ashoka, Shershah, and Akbar are as famous as those of Napoleon. In essence, the difficulty of restricting road use to toll payers made it essential for the state to step into road building.

The possibility of infection makes community hygiene an indivisible affair and the legitimate province of government; so is pollution control.

The benefits of flood control are independent of the contribution of the individual beneficiary, while, in large-scale irrigation, the upstream populations are in a position to impose on those living downstream losses for which the latter can extract no compensation. The practical importance of large-scale water control in semi-arid areas is now widely recognized—thanks to Wittfogel's (67) analysis of 'hydraulic despotisms' based on major irrigation. The watershed principle in the demarcation of national boundaries is founded on the natural political unity of any river basin.

In technical progress, external economies accrue because of the limited appropriability of knowledge. The consequent inability of the inventor to capture much of the fruits of his work would seriously deter research but for patent systems operated by the state. Where, indeed, rapid diffusion of innovations is also desired, the state may instead subsidize technical progress. And, while the interest of most governments in supporting research is a recent phenomenon, we do indeed have parallels from antiquity. Archimedes' dealings with his princely patron in Syracuse may be apocryphal; the prizes offered by sixteenth-century western European governments for an accurate method of determining longitude at sea are not.

In education, the prime beneficiary of the learning process is the trainee; but he may not be able to pay for his training out of current income and prospective lenders to him would be discouraged by the fact that, in a non-slave society, such credit would have the character of an unsecured loan. State support of education is a logical corollary—especially in societies where the returns on skills are high compared to those on unskilled labour. The densely populated backward economies of today are good examples.

Full employment in the Keynesian sense is another external economy requiring political guarantees. It is a major preoccupation of contemporary governments in the advanced West.

The mercantilist use of national trading monopolies to manipulate the terms of trade against foreigners has a long history from the chartered companies of the Renaissance to the state trading corporations of today.

The pervasiveness of external economies in development has not yet been explicitly appreciated in full, despite the formulations of Nurkse (43), Rosenstein-Rodan (52), Scitovsky (56), and others. But policy as usual has long overtaken theory; indeed, as examples like that of Petrine Russia show, the state's role in economic development is now a matter of ancient history.

The contractualist viewpoint, then, focuses on the harmony of interests within the community. It views the state as a mechanism for achieving Pareto-optimality in the presence of external effects. But it goes further. For, Pareto-optimality merely implies that none can be made better off without worsening someone else's position. It does not mean that everyone is better off or at least as well-off as a result of the operation of the state—an implication that underlies the contractualist approach. The latter contractualist postulate is, of course, legitimate only where individuals or groups can opt out of the state with impunity. It does not hold in the vast majority of cases, for such freedom is a rare luxury indeed.

The Conflict Model of the State
The appropriate political model for most communities is power-political, not contractualist. The state here is best regarded as a hierarchy of power relationships, an instrument for the organized exercise of power. In this light it will appear to serve primarily the interests of the dominant and thereby to solidify and reinforce the underlying structure of authority in the society. This, indeed, is the Marxian interpretation of the state—as the instrument of exploitation of the mass by the ruling élite. But power and conflict are the dominant motifs of a more ancient tradition of political thought, dating back at least to Hobbes (30) and continued today by thinkers like Dahrendorf (8).

How do the consequences of this model of conflicting interests compare with those of the contractualist harmony-of-interests thesis? I suggest that, even in a highly stratified state, there are in the nature of things constraints on the power of the dominant which limit the extent of exploitation possible.

First, the power of the strong is limited by the technological necessity of enlisting the co-operation of the weak. Many productive inputs simply cannot be extracted by coercion—initiative and enterprise for example or skills of the non-quantifiable kind. Even where assets can be forced out of their holders in the first instance, their renewal cannot always be compelled. Slaves, for instance, may not reproduce and capital levies might annihilate the incentive to save. The limit that this sets on dominance will be stricter, the more indispensable the services of the weak, and the scarcer their supply in relation to demand. A highly elastic supply produced by expanding conquests in the early phases of colonization, for instance, leads to more intense exploitation. Likewise, if the strong are relatively independent of the co-operation of the weak, the asymmetrical relationship of dominance would be reinforced.

The second constraint on dominance arises from the cost of maintaining it. On the one hand, power has to be defended against the challenge of rival élites, external and internal. On the other, it has to be wielded in the face of the resistance of the exploited. The higher the intensity of exploitation, the stronger the temptation to rival power-seekers and the incentive of the exploited to resist. However, the costs of maintaining control can be reduced by inculcation of a proper ideology; this would be a system of thought which justifies the rules by which society operates and thus provides a rationale for the *status quo*. The ideology would arise and be perpetuated in part through a conscious programme directed by an élite and in part through the automatic process of acculturating new generations to the dominant values in society. The acculturation process is essentially costless to the élite once the ideology has been accepted. In this way, the bulk of a society may be reconciled to a low standard of living or to vast inequalities in the distribution of income or of power, if these correspond to the ideologically justified hierarchic structure of society.

All the same, the power of illusion is limited if contradicted by actual experience. In particular, while the masses may remain quite content with a low standard of living if they know no better, contact with the dramatically superior ways of life of foreigners or prior experience of better days at home is sure to stir dissatisfaction. Rapid deterioration in levels of living thus must be avoided to minimize the resistance of the mass to the existing order; and so should exposure to superior consumption patterns. A system which failed to do this must devote a mounting fraction of its resources to an unequal struggle to maintain internal order; it will then become increasingly vulnerable to external pressure, dissolving ultimately into an anarchy which ends only with the rise of a new élite— whether from inside or out.

The State as an Equilibrium of Forces

Given these constraints on the power of the strong, the hierarchic structure of the state cannot be visualized as a model of absolute authority on the one hand and total impotence on the other. It is rather a formal arrangement for orderly decision resting on a tacit social contract, a bargaining equilibrium which averts the costs of social conflict. In the bargaining, those who are more independent and those who are most needed by others technologically are, of course, at an advantage, but the web of technology does not leave room for total independence anywhere.

All this has two implications. First, since the state—whatever its formal structure—cannot completely ignore the interests of any of its permanent members, it tends to explore Pareto-optimal solutions. Secondly, while the state has distributive powers, these are limited not only by the formal political structure but also by the underlying bargaining equilibrium. The existence of an organized political apparatus, and the fact of formal legitimacy are, of course, sources of power in themselves. But this power cannot long survive conflict with the technological necessities reflected in the underlying bargaining equilibrium.

The state, then, must function as an instrument of collective action by the community for common material goals. But this function tends to determine its political configuration (i.e. its power structure). Changes in the material and technological environment call for changes in the distribution of authority. If the political system is too rigid to respond, the consequence is revolution.

The Process of Taste-formation as a Conservative Factor in the Political Equilibrium

If the state is founded on such a bargaining, or game-theoretic, equilibrium, political changes must be traceable to changes in the ranking order of different strategies in the preference-scales of the players. Any analysis of such changes requires a brief excursion into psychology. The stability of an economic system depends on the degree to which it fulfils the wants of people. Wants, however, are not autonomous. They have, of course, a genetic basis in the hereditary reflexes. But genetic heritage counts for little in man. The human brain and nervous system at birth are infinitely more immature—relative to their adult states—than those of any other animal. The bulk of the human brain grows and most of the paths and interconnections of the nervous system form long after birth, when external stimuli are already reaching them. Hence the prolonged dependence of the human infant on his environment, his vast capacity for learning, and the unique role of experience, particularly early experience, in moulding him.

The personality of the individual, then, is largely a product of his environment. Moreover the links between personality traits and what the economist knows as behaviour or wants are rarely direct. They are forged by a chain of associations developed through repeated experience. Wants are learned, not innate. They are not instinctual, but culturally conditioned.

An example of the extent to which wants are learned in a process of social acculturation is the fact that, even in so instinctual a matter as the search for food, societies differ enormously—not only in what they find pleasant but also in what they consider to be food at all.

Think of the sacred cows and the taboos, whether of primitive tribalism or of modern civilization.

The culturally conditioned character of wants is the basis of the advertising industry. Indeed, commercial advertising is exactly complementary to normal cultural contacts in stimulating wants. It concentrates on new sophisticated differentiated products because old and standardized commodities are familiar enough through ordinary social intercourse. It aims at high income groups and affluent societies because of the visible example set by these to poorer people and countries.

The point that *some* wants are socially generated is not of course a novel one at all. The Veblen–Duesenberry–Nurkse–Galbraith tradition in economics is dominated by precisely this theme. What needs emphasizing nevertheless is the universality and pervasiveness of the demonstration effect in colouring the *entire* spectrum of human wants. From earliest infancy, a process of social selection is at work on our impulses, encouraging those which are compatible with our environment, deflecting those which are not into socially sanctioned channels. Wants are thus adapted to reality; for few individuals are likely to persist throughout the prolonged dependence of childhood in fruitless and socially disapproved desire for what is altogether inaccessible.

A closed and static economic environment generates, therefore, a stable structure of wants; indeed, it maintains an equilibrium in which it generates only those wants which it is capable of fulfilling.

Forces of Change in the Political Equilibrium

The equilibrium is disturbed only when its capacity to satisfy the long-established scale of wants is suddenly impaired. This condition is usually produced by rising population pressure on an inelastic resource base; the abruptness of the change may result either from an explosion of numbers in a population hitherto stagnant or from the sudden appearance of natural resource constraints in an expanding economy.

An open environment is exposed to three other sources of change. First, it may be penetrated by alien influences which create new wants—a 'revolution of rising expectations' or 'international demonstration effect' *à la* Nurkse (43) which is a function of its contact with the outside world. This involves a change in tastes. But the pay-off structure of an open society may also change due to

external factors. There may be changes in external earning opportunities which would change the relative attractiveness of different
kinds of socio-political organization. There may be fluctuations in
external military pressure.

Of course, these forces do not impinge uniformly on all participants in an institutional order. There is rarely, if ever, a unity of
interests in institutional change, but rather a tumult of conflicting
pressures. As the forces we have described intensify and percolate
from class to class, they produce a gradual shift in the balance of
pressures. Certainly, however, until they emerge, the adaptation of
wants to the realities of early life acts as a conservative influence on
the social framework.

The mere emergence of a popular desire for change does not
guarantee a response by the government. A degree of political
inertia is inevitable, since elements of the élite will be deeply
committed to the old order. But if—as I have suggested—the state is
based on an equilibrium of forces, it cannot ignore the demands for
change without loss of political stability. As control of discontent
and defence against external threats absorb an increasing proportion of its resources, the authority of the state melts away, leaving it
vulnerable to revolution or invasion.

The major exception to all this is the state which maintains its
authority through the overwhelming military support of a foreign
super power. Such is the classic *comprador* state visualized in the
Marxian doctrine of neo-colonialism—a state which is shielded
from internal and external pressures for development. Even in such
a state, however, the scale of external support for the élite will be
proportionate to the interest of the foreign power in the survival of
the élite. It will not increase without limit to contain a rising tide of
discontent—but will be stepped down and withdrawn as the protection of the super power's interest become costlier.

A ruling élite may thus cease to find its earlier policies worthwhile; it will then be prepared to pay the price of reform or at least
the costs of economic development—if not to satisfy popular
demands, at least to consolidate the logistic base for their suppression. Élites which fail to adapt adequately in this fashion will be
forcibly overthrown.

Political change, as I have outlined it, is not primarily a revolutionary process. Revolutions have a role in sweeping away the more
intransigent elements of the old order which are incapable of the

adaptations that the new age requires. But they are mere episodes in a continuum of gradual change in the balance of power. There is little inevitability about a revolution. What precipitates it is in fact a miscalculation of the opposition by one or more of the contenders in a revolutionary struggle.

The direction in which a political system evolves is, however, more predictable than the manner in which it changes. In fact, I have outlined essentially the driving forces behind this evolution. Where these forces come up against institutional and psychological rigidities stresses and tensions accumulate which may require a violent resolution.

Two Examples From History

The pages to follow will abound in examples of the political processes outlined. The present chapter limits itself to two illustrations remote enough in time to permit a measure of perspective: one from the history of classical Greece, the other from that of medieval Christendom.

Population Pressure, Export Opportunity, and the Rise of Athenian Democracy

Greece in the Iron Age, as is well known, was beset by continuous demographic pressure. Her swelling population overflowed abroad in colonization and settlement all around the shores of the Mediterranean and the Black Sea. But by the seventh and sixth centuries BC the expansion of the Hellenic world was approaching the territorial limits that it could hold against the opposition of the surrounding peoples. The Malthusian problem of mainland Greece deepened. Attica, in particular, experienced a crisis of exceptional intensity due to the extreme inelasticity of her arable land area. Endowed as she was with a landscape even more rugged than that of the other Greek states, the rapid deforestation that Iron Age implements made possible and the soil erosion that ensued had reduced Attica to a mass of eroded hillsides with but a few level patches of thin soil. The pressure of population and the continued loss of her top soil combined in the sixth century to produce a volcanic social crisis. Repeated subdivision of holdings reduced the smaller peasantry to indebtedness and eventual debt-slavery, or to selling their land and joining the urban proletariat. The concentration of landownership in the aristocracy accelerated; a vertical stratification of property developed with the rich landlords monopolizing all of the relatively fertile plain and what remained of the poorer peasantry driven up the hillsides. In the towns, the rising price of food penalized handicrafts and commerce and made the urban middle class a natural ally of the rural poor.

The Athenian solution of the problem was based on the city's magnificent location for maritime commerce. Athens became a massive importer of cereals, relying on grain from Egypt, Sicily, and the Black Sea coast for fully 80 per cent of her requirements. It paid for the imports by developing industry, mining, and cash-crop cultivation for export. The rocky hillsides—once freed of the necessities of subsistence agriculture—were ideally adapted to the olive, the fig, and the vine. To the exports of wine and oil were added pottery, marble, wool, and luxury handicrafts. There was also, of course, silver from the mines at Laurium which formed the basis of the most widely-accepted currency of the Mediterranean. It was this specialized adaptation that shaped the history and politics of Athens for the next two hundred years, paved the way for her golden age, and determined her imperial destiny and eventual collapse.

But the expansion of trade on these lines was incompatible with the balance of political power in seventh-century Athens. It called for

1. a legal framework that could protect non-agricultural forms of property and mercantile contracts;
2. government investment in a navy to protect the vital Athenian trade routes;
3. public expenditure on harbour facilities;
4. a government monopoly of coinage safeguarded by government control of the Laurium silver mines;
5. above all, a power configuration which would permit a reduction in grain prices despite the losses thus imposed on the large landowner.

All this could not possibly be accomplished by an oligarchy—the landed aristocracy that dominated the kinship structure of Athenian politics up to the sixth century. But, between the election of Solon to the archonship in 594 BC and the completion of Cleisthenes' constitution-making in 502 BC, Athenian politics was radically transformed. The tribal organization of the state was abolished; the franchise was progressively broadened till it embraced all free-born Athenian citizens; in the most liberal tradition of participatory democracy, public offices were to be filled by lottery from among all citizens prepared to accept the responsibility. Democracy was limited, of course, not only by the exclusion of women, slaves, and resident aliens, but also by the fact that regular participation in assemblies and public offices required time and money which the poor generally could not afford. Yet there was a very real devolution of power from the rich to the poor peasantry and the urban middle class. Thus, Solon could cancel all debts; and after Pericles, power could pass in succession to a tanner, a rope seller and a lamp-maker. Meanwhile, the reconstructed state supplied the necessities of the mercantile economy that we have already detailed.

This peaceful transition was a product, on the one hand of the discontent produced by rising food prices and deepening inequalities in land ownership, and on the other of the fear of a violent revolution. Indeed, after Solon, the oligarchy reasserted itself; and the populist dictatorship of Peisistratus was needed to restore Athens to the course of democratic evolution. The rising economic power of the merchant class added to the momentum of the process; so did the perception of the wide range of economic opportunity that commercial expansion might open up. In the event, even the oligarchy reluctantly acquiesced in the curtailment of its powers— averting thereby the social holocaust that the seventh century had seemed to foreshadow.

Military Pressure and European Feudalism

If the rise of Athenian democracy is an effect of population increase in the presence of export opportunity, the growth of feudalism in the medieval West is the consequence of military pressure on a society where trade, transport, and the fiscal basis of authority are alike on the brink of extinction.

From the late Empire throughout the early Middle Ages right up to the tenth century, western Europe was dominated by wave after wave of warlike invaders. The repercussions on trade and transport have been widely debated; and while there are differences of opinion on trade within the period—the controversy involving Henri Pirenne (48), Alfons Dopsch (14), and Jean Lombard (37), for instance, on whether the Carolingian era saw a commercial revival or a recession from the Merovingian—it is virtually unanimous on two points. It is agreed that communications, commerce, and central authority were exceedingly precarious for the period as a whole and that their fluctuations were correlated with military security. Thus, the reconquest of the West by Justinian produced a renaissance for over half-a-century from his Pragmatic Sanction of 554 to the reign of Heraclius, when it was abruptly cut short by the irruption of Islam. Any possible Carolingian revival was aborted in the ninth and tenth centuries by a fresh cycle of invasions—the Saracen closure of the Tyrrhenian Sea, the Viking fleets on the northern and western coasts, and the Magyar cavalry from the East.

Two factors conditioned the West's response to these pressures. There was the primitive character of land-transport technology— which hindered the movement of goods and armies, the maintenance of authority, and the collection of taxes over any distance. Further, there was the location of the West in terms of medieval geography—at the end of the then-known world, the terminus of natural transport arteries rather than the crossroads of trade. Constantinople in contrast stood at the intersection of routes from the Dnieper, the Danube, the Mediterranean, and the Black Sea: it was the gateway between the continents, commanding the silk road from China and India, the spice caravans to Aleppo and Antioch, and the amber route through Russia. The Byzantine Empire, therefore, controlled a minimum volume of trade which, funnelled as it was through a single point, could be taxed to provide an enduring fiscal basis for its authority. No comparable focus of trade and taxable capacity existed in the West.

Even so, the agrarian economy of the western European interior could perhaps have sustained an effective central authority if there had been just one frontier to be garrisoned. A bureaucratic empire of the oriental variety may then have evolved, with a central army guarding the vulnerable border, supported by revenues collected by a far-flung bureaucratic network. The long open coastline of western Europe ruled this out. It made for a spatial dispersion of threat which rendered political centralization impossible. Thus, the Carolingians who had succeeded in containing the Germanic tribes with their Frankish infantry had no counter to the Saracen pirates and the Viking raiders from the sea. The disintegration of central authority in these circumstances was not just inevitable: it was also necessary in order to pave the way for what at the moment was a more economical security system.

This system was dominated by the great landlord, who provided law and order and security at the local level and amply recompensed himself by exactions in goods and services from the peasantry. The institution of serfdom was the medieval corollary of the tax-obligations of the citizen: the serf was tied to the feudal lord, who was at once his protector and his revenue authority. The feudal system was in this sense a concurrent decentralization of the military powers and revenue functions of government. But, since such decentralization made trade and transport even more difficult, it spelled economic decentralization as well. Local self-sufficiency—based on the great estate or *villa*—was the most distinctive feature of the manorial economy. The decay of trade meant also the eclipse of money, of towns, and of urban industry. Land became the sole source of wealth and the basis of economic power. The political, military, and economic loci of power had converged. Yet the essential role of military pressure in the evolution of feudal institutions is clear. From the eleventh century onwards, the relaxation of this pressure led to the slow growth of communications and commerce, of urban life and monetary circulation, of credit and interest—eventually to the rise of nation-states and the mercantile economy.

4

NATIONAL ECONOMIC DEVELOPMENT
AS AN ADAPTIVE PROCESS

THE model of society and politics I have sketched constitutes the framework within which the purely economic aspects of adaptation can work themselves out. The present chapter extends the viewpoint of the earlier ones to the analysis of economic growth within any given society. The growth process is visualized as the society's production response to the opportunities and challenges presented by the environment. The main environmental constraint on production is the endowment of natural resources; and one way of looking at growth is in terms of shifts in the relationship between production and natural resources as the society adapts to changes in the other environmental variables.

Economic development then can be viewed as a process of continuous accumulation of pressures on the natural resource base and their resolution. This interpretation implies a certain typology of development. Growth processes may be classified according to their main motive forces—the primary sources of pressure on the resource base. Or, they may be distinguished by the different modes of resolution of this pressure.

The Motive Forces of Growth

A distinction must be drawn between the primary driving forces of growth and their secondary repercussions. The former are the autonomous impulses; the latter, the induced multiplier-accelerator processes. The primary impulses that lead to enlargement of demand are essentially of four kinds:

1. increasing exports or unilateral transfer from the rest of the world,
2. population growth,
3. demonstration effects in consumption,
4. increasing military pressure.

The role of increase in export incomes or unrequited inflows of purchasing power (whether as imperial tribute, plunder, private capital inflow,or foreign aid) in the stimulation of growth is a familiar one. But a word should perhaps be said about the other three factors.

Population growth works both through the market and through the political process to stimulate development. On the one hand, it changes initially the pattern of private consumption (as distinct from the *level*) leading to increased demand for food, clothing, and shelter. Given the differences in input requirements, these demands cannot be fully met at unchanged prices by simply diverting resources released by the contracting sectors. Scarcities therefore appear, prices rise, and innovations are eventually induced—thus ultimately increasing income and effective demand. On the other hand, population growth depresses standards of living (at least until it induces technical progress); it thereby generates discontent and political pressures for government action in the interests of development. Esther Boserup (5) has suggested that the major innovations in the history of agriculture were consequences rather than causes of population growth—an opinion widely disputed more on grounds of logic than of fact. The mechanism I have described provides perhaps an analytic justification for the Boserup thesis.

The demonstration effect of new goods and ways of life operates similarly on two levels. By making higher incomes more attractive, it stimulates private work and saving effort. This, of course, is an effect on the supply, rather than the demand, side. At the same time, however, it generates political demands for higher incomes— and for expanding outlets for the increasing flow of savings and willing workers. It dictates, therefore, a government policy of economic development through increased demand.

Finally, armament in response to increasing military pressure directly increases the demand for public goods. It stimulates research for a superior technology of war and better logistics of communications and supplies—affecting demands throughout the country. In many senses, this is perhaps the most compelling factor of all, since the survival of the society itself is put at stake.

A fifth major stimulant of growth could have been technical progress, and certainly induced innovation has a central role in *sustaining* development—which I shall examine later. Learning from foreign models may also play a part in *initiating* development, though here its role cannot readily be disentangled from the other aspects—referred to above—of contact between cultures. I do not, however, believe that autonomous innovation can readily appear in a sheltered and stagnant economic backwater; and for this reason I do not reckon it among the *prime* movers of development—a point that I elaborate later.

The Concept of Prime Movers of Development

One should pause at this point to reflect on a methodological issue. Since growth, once under way, is a circular cumulative process, how, it may be asked, could one isolate certain forces as primary? Did the chicken come first, after all, or the egg? Is a particular factor exogenous to the growth of a given society or is it endogenous?

I have tried to identify those forces as primary which might emerge *even in a long-stagnant economy,* and may therefore provide the initial impetus for development. Some of these forces would reflect the intrusion of other societies or the impact of technological and economic developments in the international economy. Others might be internally generated even in a closed and otherwise static environment; population in particular may begin to increase even amidst general stagnation because of the precariousness of social controls on its growth—a point I elaborate in the next chapter.

Undoubtedly, however, development produces a feedback on some of these prime movers. It may accelerate population growth, for instance. It may produce learning effects or economies of scale which add to export potentials. Where the development process is outward-looking, it may intensify demonstration effects or even military conflicts with one's neighbour. At the moment, however, I am discussing not so much the internal logic of growth as the reinforcement it derives from factors exogenous to the growth process (though not necessarily to the relevant society). It is on the exogenous component of the motive forces referred to above that I focus. The analogues I have in mind for growth would be models of adaptation to environmental change or physico-chemical systems which inevitably dissipate energy and can be sustained only by renewed energy input. The best-known economic model of this kind is Hicks's trade-cycle, with autonomous investment as its sustaining input, or driving force.

Obviously, the relative importance of the motive forces would vary between different societies and periods. No generalizations on this account are possible. Indeed, one of the principal purposes of this book is to show how differences in these motive forces affect the growth paths of different societies.

Migration as a Response to the Motive Forces

Of the four motive forces for growth, export expansion constitutes an opportunity while the other three are pressures that induce economic development primarily through the political process. An alternative response to these pressures is migration. Which of the two responses is the likelier depends, among other things, on the degree of international mobility. Migration comes easily to the nomad but it is alien to the way of life of a sedentary civilization. Far more important, however, than the migrant's reluctance to move is the resistance of recipient societies to immigration. This varies inversely with the excess demand for labour in the host country. Surges of rapid growth reduce the hostility to immigration, but there almost always persists the incentive to restrict any mass influx that would reduce, or retard the growth of, local living standards.

Ancient and medieval history is a long chronicle of mass transfers of population, particularly of waves of nomadic conquest and invasion. The nineteenth century, too, had its mass migrations—from western Europe to the New World—migrations which were crucial in sustaining at least the Irish and Swedish economies. But, in a world of closed frontiers and sovereign states, the economic role of migration is likely to be severely limited and politically forced development may, in fact, be a line of lesser resistance. By the same token, when insuperable natural resource barriers to development emerge, the pressure to migrate increases.

Patterns of Developmental Response

The richer the natural resource endowment—the larger the volume and elasticity of natural resources—the more smoothly will demand pressures induce growth. If, however, the pressures are sustained, scarcities will sooner or later emerge. The resolution of these shortages may follow any of three courses

First, if there is an elastic external supply of locally scarce natural resource products, imports would mount. Growth would be transmitted abroad: the marginal propensity to import would rise, reducing the domestic multiplier effects of any expansionary forces.

If, however, foreign as well as local supplies are inelastic, the pressures on natural resources either induce innovation or erode and eventually extinguish growth. Innovations have a long gestation lag. They require a period of research and experiment which is longer the larger the technological discontinuity involved. So a temporary check to growth is almost inevitable. However, if the long-run expansionary forces are sustained,the economy is driven against the natural resource barrier again and again. Ultimately, either the necessary innovations emerge or society regulates the expansionary factors in order to avoid being destroyed in a series of Malthusian disasters.

The impact of the induced innovations is rather uncertain. There is reason to think that they would involve substitution of the more abundant domestic resources for scarce ones. However, it is not impossible that their primary effect would be the replacement of scarce resources by factors which are more abundant abroad than at home. In the latter case, the result would be diffusion of growth abroad through rising imports. In the former, however, domestic expansion of output, income, and demand would be revived. The circular process of sustained growth would work for a while, unconstrained by natural resource shortages.

A qualification should be added here about my treatment of imports as leakages from growth. It may be argued that imports would have to be paid for in the long run by exports, and that this concurrent expansion of imports and exports would generate the gains of international specialization to the benefit of the growth process. This is certainly possible on occasion. Growth in import demand may induce economies of scale or technological innovations in the transportation or production of the import. The terms of trade of the importing country then may not deteriorate at all: they may even improve. The extreme example of this is where the growing demand for some product draws a new region into the orbit of international trade with the indivisible infra-structure of knowledge and other overheads being established. The nineteenth-century relationship between western Europe and the United States is, of course, the classic case in point. In general, however, an expanding demand for imports can be fulfilled only by exporting at deteriorating terms of trade; and growth impulses do therefore drain away.

The taxonomy of my analysis is illustrated by the chart, below:

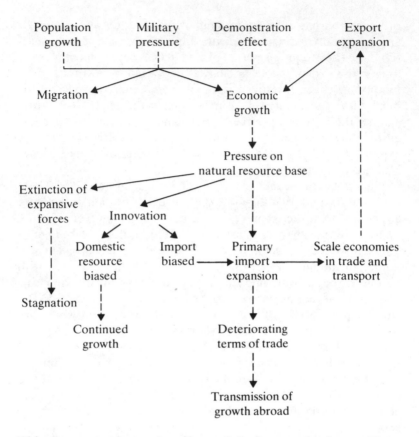

This does not exhaust the effects of the four motive forces. Thus, military pressure may lead to improvements in weapons and tactics, uncorrelated with politico-economic change, population pressure to contraception. But there will always be *some* pressure in the directions indicated. The distribution of the burden of adjustment will depend on the relative institutional and technological rigidities in each direction.

It is worth emphasizing again that I do not imply unidirectional causation. In fact, I fully appreciate the presence of feedback effects. The chart is thus constructed only to focus on the crucial role in our model of the exogenous *component* in our motive forces. Growth processes in my analysis tend to extinguish themselves against natural resource barriers—except in the unlikely event of the necessary innovations appearing immediately. They are then revived by the autonomous demand factors, which drive the economy against the natural resource ceiling again and again—until the required innovations do emerge.

The Causes of Stagnation

This approach to development implies a certain perspective on stagnation. Economies may stagnate because of:

1. the absence of any expansionary forces;
2. the overflow of expansionary pressures abroad in mounting primary imports without an offsetting growth in external demand;
3. inelasticities of both foreign and domestic supply of natural resources which innovation is unable to surmount.

In addition, there is the transient stagnation that results from lags in response to expansionary forces. Particularly where the expansion process must be mediated by government, the inertia of the political system in adapting to its necessities may impose a major, if temporary, check on development.

Stagnation due to the second and third factors above might lead eventually to stagnation of the first variety as the expansionary impulses are extinguished to avert a Malthusian calamity. A society must do two things to throttle the forces of change. First, it must adopt devices for controlling population density; thus, all isolated primitive communities practise abortion and infanticide extensively, while some of the more highly organized of them also indulge in such exotic refinements as mass-sacrifice. Secondly, the society must insulate itself from the military pressures, demands, and demonstration effects of the outside world—wherever such isolation is not enforced anyway by geography. Consider for example the self-imposed isolation of Tokugawa Japan for two hundred and fifty years.

Such measures may stabilize a society well within the Ricardian limit with an element of slack to absorb random shocks. An ecological equilibrium would thus be achieved which might endure for a very long time. It cannot, however, be permanent. The population, for one thing, is likely eventually to resume its growth because of man's instinctual urge to reduce mortality while resisting any cuts in family size. Even if it does not, the outside world will sooner or later invade one's retreat; and the long period of withdrawal and stagnation will make it impossible for the society to defend its solitude. A new cycle of expansion will then be initiated.

Innovation and the Growth Process

The classical basis of this approach is Ricardian. It is the proposition that growth with a given technology and inelastic natural resources leads to diminishing returns and eventually a stationary state. Diminishing returns here are a corollary of almost any plausible technology; all that is necessary is indispensability of natural resources in the mild sense of production being impossible in their total absence. The stationary state finale—as distinct from indefinite growth at a diminishing rate—requires a little more by way of assumptions. Any of the following will do:

1. A minimum depreciation rate of capital and minimum subsistence requirements for labour would impose an outer limit on growth.
2. A positive rate of time preference would set a floor to the return on capital at which incentive to save vanishes.
3. A liquidity trap at a positive interest rate would annihilate investment incentives even if the desire to save is maintained.

At any rate, if growth within a given technology is self-limiting, technical change must be recognized as the secret of sustained growth. Unfortunately, there is no rigorous theory of the determinants of technical progress. The Kennedy–Weiszacker (32,61) analysis of the innovation possibility frontier—whatever its merits—relates to the direction of innovation rather than its rate. Indeed, there are excellent reasons why no rigorous explanation of technological change may ever be possible.

However, evidence has been mounting that innovation is primarily an economic activity. The empirical work of Schmookler (55), Griliches (20), and Mansfield (39) suggests that the rate of innovation is a function of the size of the market. This Adam Smith-like proposition has a plausible economic rationale: the wider the market for any industry, the higher the returns on the research cost of an invention relating to it; the stronger, therefore, the incentive to innovate.

A corollary of this view of innovation is the abandonment of the myth of autonomous technical progress, falling manna-like from heaven or from the ivory towers of absent-minded scientists.

Hence, autonomous innovation is not given a place among the primary propellants of growth. Of course, any region might benefit from the impact on the demand pattern of its goods of innovations induced by economic pressures elsewhere—but that is a different story.

The rising pressure of demand on inelastic but indispensable natural resources, then, must set the stage for induced resource-saving innovation. For, while the tempo of technical progress is limited by the size of the market, its direction is set by factor scarcities. The explanation of this lies in the proportionality of the marginal rates of return on investment in augmenting particular factors to the respective factor shares. If a factor is relatively irreplaceable within the existing technology, if its elasticities of substitution with respect to other factors are less than unity—as seems likely with natural resources—a rise in its price would raise the rate of return on technical progress which augments it and induce more research with this objective. It is sometimes claimed that there are increasing returns to concentration of research in a particular direction (Nordhaus (42)). If this were so, research would be discontinuously switched from efforts to augment one factor exclusively to efforts to augment another as the relative share of the latter rises above a critical level.

An alternative view of innovation—as essentially the product of Arrovian learning by doing—has been argued brilliantly and force-fully by Paul David (10). This is not necessarily in conflict with the concept of demand-induced innovation. The larger the market for an industry, the larger the output and the stronger the learning effects. However, the relative neglect of *anticipated*, as distinct from past, demand as an influence on the rate of innovation is peculiar to the learning theory. Empirically, this may not be a testable difference, with expectations being a function of past experience. In this sense, choice between the two alternative views of innovation may not be a terribly meaningful exercise. However, if one insists on a definite choice between the two models of inno-vation, I would be inclined to attach more weight to that of demand-induced technical progress. My reasons are two. First, without denying the importance of learning processes and continuities in the engineering design of improvements, I feel that most major inno-vations involve drastic discontinuities, radical shifts in technological perspective for which day-to-day experience of the established technology is not necessarily the ideal preparation. Students of the inventive process (e.g. Koestler (33)) stress the role in it of the synthesis of ideas drawn from unrelated, often very widely disparate, fields: this would seem to call, not for a commitment to existing production methods, but perhaps for a certain distance from them. Secondly innovation is very largely the product of investment in research—rather than of the costless absorption of experience; and Schmookler's demand approach focuses far better on this investment and its profitability.

Natural Resources as a Supply Constraint

Why the central role of natural resource scarcity as a supply constraint on development?

First, supply functions of other inputs shift outwards over time—even with a static technology—due to population growth and capital formation. On the other hand, land, the basis of renewable resources, has a fixed supply function and the supply curves of exhaustible resources shift inwards with time. The limits to growth set by labour and capital supply recede with time even in a technologically static world. The natural resource barrier does not.

The two forces that temper the pressure of factor scarcities on growth are economies of scale and technological change (including new resource discoveries). These may be neutral in their impact effect on technology, and operate by reducing the cost of production of the scarce factor—scale economies or inventions in the primary sector or the capital goods sector, for instance. Or they may economize on its use directly—as in the case of 'biased' technical progress.

Scale economies, however, though almost universal in industry, have but a marginal role in agriculture. Given an infinitely elastic supply of inputs to the production unit, every production process which is amenable to standardization tends towards increasing returns. The crucial factor here is the frequency with which entrepreneurial decision-making is required. A process that depends on the continuous exercise of managerial judgement cannot be reduced to a mechanical sequence of standard operations. The growth of output increases the strain on the decision-making capacities of the enrepreneur and limits the scope of increasing returns. This is the key to the technological differences between agriculture and industry. One is a biological production process with all its random variability, the other a mechanical one. One is subject to the infinite variety of natural conditions, the vagaries of the weather, the subtle variation of soil and slope; the other largely independent of such uncontrollable elements. In the most important segment of the primary sector, then, increasing returns offer little relief from factor supply constraints on growth. Any expansion process encounters diminishing returns in agriculture almost from its very outset— while industry is still exploiting scale effects.

In a market economy, this difference in response between agriculture and industry is heightened by the difference in their market structures. Increasing returns lead to the domination of industry by oligopoly, while agriculture typically remains the stronghold of competition. Growth of industrial demand, therefore, is accompanied by the assimilation of unused innovations which the oligopolists had not exploited in a stagnant market for fear of depressing prices. Increase in agricultural demand, on the other hand, cannot mobilize such untapped technological potential; for agriculture— being more competitive—would anyway have deployed all innovations that are profitable at current prices. A similar point is the likely presence of excess capacity in industry but not in agriculture at the outset of an expansion.

All this does not imply a lower rate of long-run technical progress in agriculture. On the contrary, innovations in the primary sector (as well as those that economize on natural resource use) have a pivotal role in our analysis. But research is induced only by buoyant demand and high prices; and research inevitably has a gestation lag—so that, in the absence of a stock of unused innovations, short-run expansion processes run rapidly into supply bottlenecks in agriculture.

Growth and Cycles

The differences in supply elasticities, scale effects, and technological responses between industry and the primary sector set the rhythm of growth in any economy where both exist. A development boom—whether set off by our autonomous motive forces or by endogenous mechanisms—generates scale economies in manufactures. A Schumpeterian wave of investment and innovation spreads through the industrial sector. As it gains momentum, it generates expectations of further growth in demand, leading to secondary waves of new investment.

Industrial expansion increases demand for food and primary materials, forcing up their prices and stimulating investment in the primary sector. But, in the absence of a new primary technology, diminishing returns set in. Rising food prices drive up wages and this, coupled with increasing raw material prices, begins to erode the rate of profit on industrial investment. At some point of this primary price spiral, research into methods of coping with natural resource scarcities becomes profitable; but, since such research would have a long gestation lag, output is not immediately affected. Meanwhile, the falling profitability of industry reduces industrial investment and demand in a multiplier-accelerator chain of deepening recession.

We have in fact a Hicksian (28) cycle, but with natural resource scarcities rather than labour shortages setting the ceiling on the boom. The lower turning-point, on the other hand, could have either of two possible causes: if research stimulated by high primary prices during the last boom is successful, the resulting innovations will be immediately deployed by the primary sector, raising its output and depressing its prices. Real incomes, therefore, rise, stimulating industrial demand, while raw material prices and perhaps wages are falling. A fresh expansion will thus be initiated, ascending to possibly unprecedented heights since the natural resource constraints on earlier booms have been eased by innovations. If, on the other hand, research is unsuccessful, revival will depend on our autonomous driving forces. Herein lies the essential importance of the latter. They sustain the cycle through several successive booms, until enough technical knowledge accumulates to drive the economy through the natural resource ceiling.

Population and Economic Growth

A final issue of interest is the role of population in the development process. So vast and complex, however, is the general area of interaction between demography and development that I shall confine myself to those fringes of it that are immediately relevant to my argument.

One accepts, of course that population growth may be induced by the process of general economic development through the usual mechanisms: reduced mortality and higher fertility because of better nutrition (McKeown (41)); a high marriage rate, decline in the age of marriage, and higher marital fertility because of improved earning opportunities (Habakkuk (21)). These are well known and need not be elaborated upon. More important for my argument—because sometimes disputed—are the autonomous components of population growth. The exogenous factors include:

1. secular climatic changes which could affect population growth either through their effects on production or through their effects on health and disease;
2. mutations of disease micro-organisms and carriers which could disturb the ecological equilibrium between them and the human species;
3. improvements in medical technology—particularly those developed elsewhere and imported at little cost;
4. the exchange of diseases through intensified contact between societies;
5. the acquisition—from alien societies—of new foods which could add significantly to population potentials without requiring any immediate change in economic structure;
6. fluctuations in the infra-structure of security—between war and peace or order and anarchy.

The significance of each of these factors has been widely substantiated. Thus, Huntington (31) accumulated massive evidence on long-term climatic cycles and their correlation with the harvests and epidemics (including the Black Death). Razzell (50) argues that population growth in eighteenth-century England was largely the product of reductions in small-pox mortality because of inoculation. Similar are the well-recorded contemporary consequences of the control of malaria in the tropics (in Ceylon, for instance) through DDT. Even more recent, of course, is the resurgence of malaria because of the emergence of mosquito strains that are immune to DDT. The mutations of the influenza virus—which have often affected mortality on a surprising scale—are, of course, well known. One such mutation is believed to account for the deadly strain that, in 1918–19, killed off some 14 million people in India alone. The classic example of ecological change in infective agents is, of course, the disappearance of the black rat from Europe—which is said to have led to the cessation of plague in the late seventeenth century (Hirst (29)). As for the exchange of diseases between societies, Durand (15) explains the demographic history of the seventeenth century in terms of the transfer of disease micro-organisms between continents following the navigations of the six-teenth. The fabled advent of syphilis in Europe after the return of Columbus may only have been the first fruits of a long harvest of death. On the other hand, Langer (35) traces the population explo-sion in Europe to the spread of new American foods (notably the potato) which sharply increased caloric yields per acre. Finally, war and its consequences have often been described as the greatest of all causes of death (Carr-Saunders (7)); hence, population growth is strongly influenced by security.

It may be argued that population would adjust in the long run to such exogenous shocks through various density-dependent effects. Thus, increased population pressure in a stagnant economy would increase mortality (by impairing nutrition levels and increasing political insecurity) and depress the marriage rate and marital ferti-lity (because of higher age of marriage and contraception). But these adjustment processes are painful and time-consuming; and, until they work themselves out, the incentive for innovation is maintained and enough discontent stirred up to act as a political imperative for change. How much of the burden of adjustment falls on demographic variables and how much on the technology and the political-economic order is a matter of relative speeds of adjust-ment. The larger the technological discontinuities and the more rigid the political institutions, the likelier it is that the population will have to regulate its density.

Controversy has long surrounded the question whether the self-regulating mechanisms act chiefly through mortality factors or ferti-lity control. T. R. McKeown (41) rules out the possibility of volun-tary control of population density without modern contraception. He concedes the pervasiveness of infanticide in backward societies; he argues, however, that this is a mortality factor of the same order as the Malthusian positive checks, and that actual fertility control was negligible. In support of the latter conclusion, he cites clinical evidence that abortion by traditional techniques, prolonged lacta-tion, rhythm methods, withdrawal, and other traditional ways of contraception are quite unreliable in averting births. He also be-lieves that postponement of marriage has little effect on marital fertility and that eventual marriage is almost universal in all tradi-tional societies. While McKeown writes brilliantly on mortality factors, his analysis of fertility is surprisingly weak. Traditional birth controls, for instance, might be unreliable for the individual, yet, when employed on a large scale, they may affect birth rates very significantly. Indeed, Henry (26) argues that their effectiveness—even for the individual couple—improves dramatically as the desired family size is approached, simply because the couple is then more strongly motivated. As for factual evidence, McKeown dismisses the accounts of anthropologists and travellers in primitive societies, and ignores family reconstitution studies like Henry's work on the Genevan bourgeoisie. Of course, French registration data, from their very beginning in 1800, reveal a continuous fall in birth rates massive enough to swamp improvements in registration—that, too, long before modern contraception, and in a Catholic country where artificial contraceptives were taboo. McKeown cannot wish this evidence away, but writes as if it is irrelevant to the experience of other countries. In sexual matters, presumably the French have a secret.

Wrigley (69, 70) is not so cavalier in dismissing the possibility of voluntary control of numbers in traditional societies. He adduces substantial evidence of family limitation and reduced marriage rates in pre-industrial communities.

I believe that stagnant societies do try with a measure of success to stabilize themselves within the Malthusian limit through fertility control. Such stability is quite imperfect, however. This is not only a matter of the voluntary checks on fertility being quite precarious (for reasons spelled out in chapter 6). The Malthusian limit itself shifts unpredictably due to envoronmental change—so that the likelihood of collision with it can be reduced, but never eliminated.

So much for the demographic adjustment to stagnation. More complex, often, is the demographic response to growth. In some environments, an increase in economic opportunities will simply induce population growth. In others it will lead to a rise in living standards as well. The crucial factor is the family-size decision. Will families respond to better economic opportunities by increasing their size (this may simply result from a passive maintenance of birth rates in the face of falling infant mortality); or will they absorb some of the benefits of growth in higher consumption per head? How does a larger size compare with higher living standards in the family's preference pattern? The key determinant of this is often the demonstration effect. When new wants are being created in a society—usually in the process of trade itself—export-induced growth must involve some satisfaction of these: it will, therefore, have an intensive rather than a purely extensive character. On the other hand, mental insulation of a society from the outer world leads to inelastic wants and a highly elastic population in the long run. An interesting example of such a society is Thailand from the 1860s to the Second World War. Separated from the main arteries of international trade by the protruding length of the Malay peninsula, Thailand during this period was never deeply penetrated by western influence and example. She developed a fast-growing export trade in rice which was handled by foreigners: but these foreigners were Chinese and set few visible consumption targets for the local population to aim at. In consequence, the Thais stagnated in serene contentment. The expansion of rice acreage and export was matched by a proportional growth of population, while standards of living remained virtually static. Of course, the Second World War, the GIs, and Vietnam changed the picture altogether.

A Recapitulation

I may sum up my argument so far as follows. All living communities in a new environment tend to expand rapidly towards the limiting size that the environment can support. As they come up against these limits they evolve biologically: natural selection between mutations of any species so changes its genetic base as to enable it to explore a different aspect of its environment and thus continue its growth. However, if no successful mutation emerges for a ling time, the species develops regulatory mechanisms which stabilize its size well within the Malthusian limits. I have shown that economic growth reflects the same processes—with innovation taking the place of adaptive mutatuion. The forces making for rapid expansion may, of course, work through the market; but their thrust is often through the political process. Innovations appear when this expansion slows down under the pressure of environmental scarcities— and their effect is to renew the momentum of growth. Finally, where the necessary innovations are far beyond the technological capacity of a society, the latter develops, in the long run, political and social controls on expansion; it ensures thereby its survival well within the Malthusian limits of its old ecological niche.

5

ALTERNATIVE PATTERNS OF NATIONAL ECONOMIC DEVELOPMENT

THE preceding chapter sought to establish a common framework for the analysis of growth processes. The present chapter traces the consequences of the differential incidence of the prime movers of development in different economies. At this point it may be worthwhile to turn back for a closer look at the mechanism through which the four motive forces of growth stimulate demand expansion. Typically, an economy which benefits from a large export market or substantial capital inflow can develop through the free play of market forces; buoyant profit opportunities would induce investment up to the limits imposed by natural resources. Economies which lack such assets would either not develop rapidly or depend massively for development on government demand or intervention in the market. Government, of course, is no *deus ex machina*, stepping in whenever needed for the salvation of the development process. On the contrary, it must be driven to act by powerful forces within the society: and I suggest that the three forces which could do this are population growth, demonstration effect, and military pressure. The responsiveness of states to these forces varies; it is a matter of the relative rigidity of defferent political structures—which, in turn, are legacies from the past and reflect, therefore, the political, military and economic conditions of an earlier era. This question—of the differential responsiveness of alternative political systems to our motive forces—is discussed at length in Part Two of this book in the context of specific examples. For the present, we focus only on the implications of differential impact of the motive forces.

The Causes of Growth in External Earnings

The best-known propellants of growth are export expansion and unilateral transfers. Export demand may expand due to the growth of population and *per capita* income in the rest of the world to an extent dependent on the income-elasticity of demand for the good in question. These forces are pervasive—impinging on all exports and all regions—if not equally strong everywhere. But, because their impact is so diffuse, the growth of trade that they bring about is everywhere of roughly the same order of magnitude as the very slow tempo of general economic evolution.

A more dramatic growth of exports would result from their capturing the markets of competing products; the latter might be effectively eliminated by scarcity, technological change, or political-military coercion, so that an intense concentration of demand results for the product of the relevant region. Such concentration would be accentuated by economies of scale in the export activity, which tend to magnify the effects of small advantages. Where a population growth effect and an income effect reinforce this substitution process, the resulting growth of the region's exports may be truly explosive.

Transport innovations are particularly important in producing such concentrations. Each transport technology is associated with a network of feasible routes and nodal points more or less rigidly prescribed by geography. Sometimes, of course, no such well-defined route systems exist and transport conditions are uniform over a large bounded area; here the central point of the area has a unique significance. Nodality or centrality attract a high density of traffic through certain points; and, given the economies of scale in transport, this makes freight reduction possible – thus attracting even more traffic. Banking and insurance also enjoy economies of scale at such locations, which become, therefore, major exporters of commercial services. Further, the transport advantage tends to attract all activities involving procurement or distribution over a distance. Extensive markets can be catered to and large supply areas exploited from such sites at a minimum cost. Thus, major changes in transport technology almost always generate new foci of economic activity.

An example of historical interest concerns Britain's role as the purveyor of shipping and commercial services to the western world from the late seventeenth, to the early twentieth century. This was a role based on her unique locational advantages in the age of ocean navigation and expanding international trade. But it was reinforced by the forcible elimination from the field of her only possible rivals, the Dutch, by a military policy which capitalized on Britain's strategic advantages.

Nearly as important is the development of new sources of energy.

The need for power and fuel in production and distribution is as universal as the need for transport. Hence, whenever technology has evolved cheap forms of energy that are not readily transmissible and are generated from materials which are expensive to transport, a very wide range of industries has grown up around this energy source. On the other hand, where the energy source is itself transportable at low cost, the regions of its occurrence become large-scale exporters of the primary material.

A contemporary example of such export expansion is of course that of Middle-East oil. The combined effects of world economic growth, technological change, and the increasing scarcity of equally cheap alternative energy sources have created an indispensable requirement for a highly localized factor. A market situation has thus arisen which is being exploited by a producer's monopoly.

All this is not to suggest that innovations are autonomous. In fact, each of the innovations we have discussed was induced by long sustained needs and demands in the international economy. Our concern at the moment is not with the origin of innovations but with the demands they generate for the products of particular regions through the process of export expansion.

The specific characteristics of innovations are, of course, unpredictable and their incidence on the exports of different regions accordingly random. But in one case the probabilities might be so overwhelming as to amount to virtual certainty. Where an open frontier fabulously endowed by nature is juxtaposed with a populous civilization straining against the limits of its natural resources, the premium on research and exploration which would facilitate the integration of the two is so phenomenal that rapid growth of trade between the two regions is virtually guaranteed. The development of the nineteenth-century pattern of regional specialization between industrial western Europe and the regions of recent settlement is, of course, the classic case in point. It was a process that required a sequence of innovations—the railroad, the steamship, and refrigeration among other things. But, as long as demand pressures in western Europe were sustained, creating scarcities of food and raw materials, the appearance of the appropriate innovations was assured, and the process of international division of labour continued to unfold. In general, despite the uncertainties of technical progress, the fate of regions with a rich natural resource endowment per head (or, as a rough proxy, a low density of population) is relatively predictable: they will sooner or later expand exports and join the mainstream of international trade and affluence. In the evolutionary perspective, this is part of the optimal adjustment of man as a species to nature: for optimization requires a balance between the intensities of natural resource utilization in different parts of the world—a movement ever forward from the more intensively exploited areas of the environment to the less, the virgin territory on the frontier of settlement, if not necessarily the horizon of knowledge.

Unilateral transfers are alternatives to exports as sources of foreign earnings. Of these, capital inflows are often a response to increasing profit opportunities: they are then a consequence rather than a cause of demand growth. Imperial tribute is another matter. Empires are maintained and tribute extracted ultimately by military might, which is largely a function of economic affluence; but there are other specifically strategic variables which determine military power—location, for example, or the control of resources vital to current military technology. The importance of strategic position in the geopolitics of imperialism is well known. In this context, I have touched briefly upon the example of England, and will dwell on it at length later. Rome likewise found its mathematically central position in the Mediterranean a crucial asset in empire-building in an age when navigation was confined to landlocked waters.

Foreign aid—when it is not a reflection of profit possibilities—is often linked to similar advantages of strategic locations or the possession of strategic materials. The contemporary cases of Korea, Taiwan, Pakistan, Israel, and Portugal illustrate the role of the locational principle in determining the flow of foreign aid.

The Effects of Increased External Earnings

The essence of both exports and transfers is the acquisition of claims on the rest of the world's output by a group in the relevant country. The expenditure of these receipts generates multiplier effects on income and demand at home, or—if the marginal propensity of the controlling group to import is high—abroad. The size and character of the group controlling external incomes is thus crucial. If it is a microscopic élite, its expenditure will be diversified over a wide variety of goods, each in small quantities. Such a demand pattern cannot form the basis of any large-scale domestic industry. If large-scale industries already exist abroad, they will have a cost advantage in catering to this demand. A high marginal propensity to import may result: external income will then flow back abroad without inducing development outside the export sector. Even if imports do not expand immediately—if, for instance, large-scale industries abroad are as underdeveloped as those at home—the domestic industries stimulated will belong to the small-scale luxury sector. Demand pressures will increase no doubt; but the growth process will not generate economies of scale and will not benefit from their accelerating effect. Expansion will be slowly diffused through the whole economy: it will have the character of evolutionary progress rather than Industrial Revolution.

On the other hand, if the external incomes are controlled by a substantial middle class, a large homogeneous domestic market will emerge. This could be the basis of large-scale industrialization.

The repercussions of increase in external incomes depend, therefore, on their distribution. This is a point made by a number of economists and historians of economic development in a variety of contexts (Baldwin (2), Habakkuk (22), Levin (36), Sachs (54)). What has not been so explicitly noticed is the relationship between factor proportions in the export economy and the distribution of the export income. In a private enterprise economy, the income distribution reflects the distribution of various productive resources, and their relative prices. Among productive resources, property tends under any given technology to become cumulatively concentrated in the long run. This is so because people with larger property can save a higher proportion of their income and add to their property faster than others. The tendency towards concentration of wealth is especially strong in backward economies with low *per capita* income; for here the very poor must often actually dissave to survive. Thus, if returns to property are high relative to returns to labour (the one resource which cannot be alienated in a non-slave society and which as such is not subject to concentration), the income distribution pattern tends to become highly skewed. Conversely, a high-wage economy has relatively egalitarian income distribution.

The pressure of population on resources is then in a non-slave, free-enterprise economy a major determinant of the consequences of export expansion. The populous backward country rarely branches out into diversified economic development as a result of primary export growth, though the emptier high-wage economy would acquire the basis for domestic industrialization. Of course, if export demand is large relative to the size of the economy, the input requirements of the export sector would themselves change relative factor prices. A large highly labour-intensive export industry in a small economy may substantially raise wages and widen the domestic market for industry.

In a free market, this would be the end of the story. Export-propelled development would be successful wherever export demand is large and population pressure relatively low. Institutional imperfections of the market may, however, frustrate this. Slavery, for instance, restricts the market by artificially cheapening labour even where it is scarce. So do other limitations on occupational choice of a segment of the labour force (such as legal barriers to the purchase or renting of land by imported labour). Typically, such institutions develop and flourish, first in regions with a comparative advantage in export products amenable to unskilled and rather careless labour (plantation perennials rather than annual field crops), and secondly in regions where the local population is too sparse or too uninterested in wage employment to constitute a cheap and reliable labour force.

Baldwin (2) has shown how the technological characteristics of cotton cultivation favoured a large-scale, slave-operated monoculture in the American South. This in turn retarded southern industrialization in sharp contrast to conditions in the mid-western grain belt. The Caribbean sugar and cotton plantations of the seventeenth and eighteenth centuries and the olive groves and vineyards of classical Greece and Rome likewise provided a fertile soil for slavery; and, as in the American South, the upshot was the restriction of the expansionary effects of their export growth.

The Mechanics of Growth with Stagnant External Earnings

But what if external incomes fail to work as an engine of growth? A closed system (whether of one or many economies) with static population, technology, and tastes converges rapidly under such conditions to a stationary state. Population, of course, tends continuously to rise—even if at an almost imperceptible rate; and I have suggested a market process whereby population growth might induce technical progress and the development of the economy as a whole. The painfully slow upward creep of technology in medieval Europe or Imperial China without significant political support

illustrates this process. Rapid growth, however, must await organized collective action. But the political system would be forced
down this path only by external military pressure or by the internal
forces of population growth and demonstration effect.

Patterns of Growth with Stagnant External Earnings

Assuming that the government is forced to act in the interests of
economic development, what is its likely strategy? Its actual choice
of policies will of course be dictated by the relative strengths of the
different political forces I have mentioned. There are, however,
certain general imperatives of economic growth with stagnant
foreign earnings. The most important of these is the need for
government stimulation of industrial demand. The industrial bias of
growth in such an environment follows from the logic of autarchy—
given the higher income-elasticity of demand for manufactures
(Engel's law). But the point that new demand should be injected, in
the first instance, into industry rather than agriculture is a consequence of two other factors. In part, it is a matter of the mechanics
of governmental demand expansion—the fact that government has
no direct use for food or indeed for any consumer goods.

In part, however, it reflects the deeper structural asymmetry
discussed in the previous chapter—the pervasiveness of economies
of scale in industry (compared with their peripheral role in agriculture). As noted earlier, in a market economy, the consequences of
this are accentuated by the likely persistence of surplus technological and plant capacity in oligopolistic industry but not in competitive
agriculture. Expansion of industrial demand, therefore, opens up
economies of scale and innovational opportunities, inducing an
immediate growth of real income without necessarily raising
industrial prices. Increase in agricultural demand, on the other
hand, runs quickly into diminishing returns. Its impact effect is not
primarily an increase in income, but its redistribution through
better terms of trade for agriculture. Only in the long run does the
research induced by higher agrarian prices bear fruit in innovations
which add substantially to agricultural productivity. As a development strategy, therefore, this is slower, more painful, and politically less acceptable than an increase in industrial demand.

It follows from the same reasoning that the critical limits on
agricultural growth are set by supply factors rather than demand.
Development policy in this context involves the provision of the

infra-structure of production—public goods like flood control, irrigation, and agricultural research and extension.

At the heart of the new deal, however, will be the various strategies of attack on the market problem. These fall essentially into
four classes. First, government might redistribute income in order
to create a substantial middle class as the basis of a mass consumer
market. Vast bureaucracies, large standing armies, proliferating
university establishments are thus not just the expensive luxuries of
backward governments: they follow from the logic of the demonstration effect as a propellant of growth; they reflect the common
interest of the manufacturer and the aspirant to middle-class status,
and they induce investment via an expansion of the market.

A second way of sustaining investment incentives would be
through direct fiscal support. Most of the poorer developing
economies deploy a formidable battery of tariffs, subsidies, etc. on
manufactures. The range of these far outstrips any justification that
the standard protectionist arguments might afford. They frankly
distort resource allocation in order to raise the rate of profit in the
interests of capitalist accumulation.

A third means to the same end would be the injection of government demand at strategic points of the economy. Locally, the
demand would be for those transport-oriented manufactures which
have a maximum of locationally associated linkage effects. Since
the government has no direct use for consumer goods, this implies
government investment in selected producer and intermediate
goods industries. Transport and other social overheads are important in this context; so are heavy industry complexes for which a
mineral base exists. These activities are very transport-intensive, so
that, in catering to a large local market on the basis of local
materials, domestic producers may be capable of withstanding
foreign competition. Government demands in these sectors should
have large domestic multiplier effects.

Finally, if investment decisions are not atomistic but synchro-
nized over a wide range of technically related industries, the expansion of one industry would support the market for another and
justify investment in it. Thus, extensive co-ordination of investment
decisions might be one way of sustaining investment incentives.
This is the Nurkse—Rosenstein–Rodan (43, 52) balanced growth
thesis. But a balanced pattern is not enough to make investment
profitable in an economy which has lagged behind in development.

With the advanced world progressing towards ever larger scales of production, competitiveness requires large indivisible plant in all industries which are not adequately protected by transport costs or government support. Dramatic increases in scale in a wide range of industries are implied by this strategy of growth.

Such synchronization of large-scale investment over a broad spectrum of activities has two important implications. It requires massive centralization of decisions. And it means that successful accumulation must occur in sudden large-scale bursts rather than by slow acceleration. Such development processes are initiated and dominated by large decision-making units. These include great industrial banks and massive cartels or business houses that branch out into industrial empires spanning a vast range of industries. But, above all, as the largest decision-making unit in any economy, there is the government. In the nineteenth-century European industrializations which followed the British—in the German Industrial Revolution for example—the role of banks and cartels was very important. So was the role of the Zaibatsu in Japan. However, in both these cases, the state also had a major function to fulfil; and in Russia—even before the Revolution—it was the dominant factor. In India, the complementary roles of the great business houses—the former 'managing agencies'—and the state is one of the distinctive features of the development process. The polar case—where all investment decisions are centralized in a single authority—is, of course, the socialist economy.

Further, the onset of such development processes has everywhere been marked by a sharp discontinuity in the rates of investment and growth. Historically, they have been revolutionary rather than evolutionary. In fact it is only in the context of such processes—and not, as Rostow would have us believe, of development processes in general—that the concept of a 'take-off' or a 'great spurt' of growth becomes legitimate.

Standard examples of growth processes in this class are the cases of modern Chinese, Russian, and Indian development. Population pressure was a major force in all three instances; but, while military threats were a crucial factor in Russia and China, they were outweighed in the Indian case by the demonstration effect in consumption. This difference in the relative balance of motive forces largely accounts for the significant differences in development patterns.

The Relative Backwardness Hypothesis

None of the four motive forces of growth excludes any others. A booming export economy experiences and indeed often induces a population spurt and demonstration effects which strongly reinforced demand expansion. Population in eighteenth-and nineteenth-century Britain, for example, rose steadily—accelerating in the latter period to the tempo of a demographic explosion. A revolution in tastes occurred as commerce flooded British markets with exotic goods from distant continents—tea, coffee, sugar, tobacco, cotton textiles, cocoa (for chocolate), strange new vegetables like the potato and tomato and flowering plants, to cite but the most obvious examples. Meanwhile, the military necessities of world-wide commercial and imperial supremacy dictated a certain interest in military expenditure. All three factors added to the effects of rising mercantile and imperial income in sustaining the growth process. Other European states which industrialized later than Britain were handicapped in developing exports of manufactures by their relatively late start and the consequent necessity of competing with large-scale British manufactures based on the already-developed British home market. Fortunately, this was not as yet an overwhelming obstacle. Meanwhile, they repeated Britain's demographic experience and were exposed to military pressures from countries which had industrialized earlier and to the demonstrative effect of the latter's living standards. The variations in relative strength of these two sets of forces were reflected in the varying patterns of European development. The later the onset of industrialization in a particular country, the harder it was to penetrate the tight circle of industrial exporters; the stronger, too, were the forces of population growth (fuelled by progressive improvement in food supply and medical technology), demonstration effect, and military pressure (because of ever-widening disparities in consumption levels and military capability). There was, therefore, a systematic relationship between the delay in the onset of industrialization in any country and its growth pattern. This relationship has been explored for European countries by Gerschenkron (19). But it is also discernible on a global scale—though partly obscured by the varying impact of geography. Broadly speaking, the later the process of industrialization in a particular country, the more restricted the significance of foreign trade and the wider the role of government and other large decision-making units; the larger, too, must the savings effort be, the sharper the discontinuity in the rate of growth, and the more repressive and austere the political regime. The explanation of this empirical relationship lies in the shifting balance over time of the different motive forces of growth. Generally, the later development processes have tended to approximate the pattern described above of growth with stagnant exports—though of course there have been a variety of exceptions. The exceptions typically are small countries exceptionally fortunate in natural resource endowment (the oil-exporters, for example) or commanding locational advantages which attract foreign capital whether for strategic reasons (Korea, Taiwan, Israel) or because of their potentialities as centres of service exports (Hong Kong, Lebanon, Singapore).

I have concentrated primarily on the differences between development induced by export and the market and growth propelled by the other three motive forces largely through the political process. However, differences in the relative intensities of the latter three forces also significantly affect development patterns and strategies. So do differences in natural resource endowment—while differences in inherited political structures affect the speed of response to our motive forces. These issues are elaborated upon in the specific case studies of Part Two.

6

THE INTERNATIONAL DIMENSIONS
OF DEVELOPMENT

THE growth processes of different nation states and societies fit into a global mosaic, the pattern of which is not always readily discernible from its pieces. Factors external to one region appear random in incidence from the regional viewpoint, though they would be seen as endogenous in an international perspective. The present chapter glances briefly at the broad panorama of economic growth considered as a global process.

World Growth as an Aggregative Process

The world economy—like any other closed economic system—develops under the shadow of diminishing returns. With technology static the expansion of augmentable factors (like capital and labour) against a fixed endowment of natural resources leads to a falling rate of profit (or surplus) and therefore to a continual deceleration of growth. The pace of development can be sustained only by technical progress; and the incentives for this fortunately are generated by the situation itself. The mounting pressure on scarce natural resources creates a demand for a new technology which would economize on them, or substitute abundant inputs for them, or at least increase their supply. In particular, a strong demand for transport innovations arises; for cheap transport mitigates shortages of all kinds of resources through the extension of trade. Innovations generally are induced if there is a strong and persistent enough demand for them.

It is not only technological innovation that is relevant here, but political and social innovation as well. Thus, the extension of trade may require not primarily a revolution in transport technology but the growth of an area of peace within which the structure of political authority protects the processes of exchange. Hicks (27) has described how the need of an expanding commerce for security of property and contract led to the rise of the city-state. But the same phenomenon has recurred often enough on a larger scale. Typically, it involves an enlargement of the area of authority. The initial units of authority—the states we begin with—lose some of their sovereignty to a new transcendental institution; sometimes they may lose their identity itself. This larger framework of authority may be imposed on the states by one among them, hopeful of capturing the major share of the gains from trade that would ensue. If none of the states is capable of such dominance, a consensus on the need for a sacrifice of local sovereignty is still likely to emerge— perhaps slowly and painfully after much indecisive conflict. The classic examples of imposed peace are of course the Roman and British Empires. The European Common Market illustrates the voluntary surrender of sovereignties—after the failure of Germany's attempts to impose its hegemony on a unified Europe.

Growth and the International Division of Labour

The process of development and trade expansion is accompanied by changes in the pattern of regional specialization. There are the general and diffuse effects on all exports of population and income growth and of uniform falls in transport costs. But more significant is the concentration of expansionary impulses in small areas induced by technical changes that create indispenable requirements for highly localized factors—changes that give certain regions a unique advantage in production or distribution. The concentration of export activity that results in these regions depends on:

1. the rigidity of the need for local factors: a resource with few substitutes will induce stronger localization than one with many;
2. the distribution of these factors over space: mineral deposits, because of their narrow spatial incidence, attract denser concentrations of activity than cheap agricultural land;
3. their mobility: the immovable facts of geography—of climate, soil, and relief (as in specialized agriculture), of geology (as in mining), and of position (as in nodal points on natural transport arteries)—provide a stronger basis for concentration than an abundance of transferable resources (like capital and labour).

Some of the focal points of the world economy then owe their status to localized 'supply' advantages. Given current technology, these are primarily a matter of positional and resource geography. But there are other nodes in the web of international exchange which attract productive activity mainly because of high local income and demand. This, in turn, may be the product of current 'supply' advantages or the legacy of past growth. The activities which are drawn to such markets are dominated typically by economies of scale and yield a product that is relatively expensive to transport. Much of modern manufacturing falls into this class.

This division of labour—with supply-oriented activities gravitating to regions of geographic advantage and market-oriented production drawn towards the affluent economies—leaves little room for the poor country which is hard-pressed for natural resources. The established rich specialize in manufacturing, the thinly populated frontier in primary exports. The poor and densely populated region can do neither and remains essentially marginal to the whole system.

The resulting inequalities could, of course, have been resolved by free factor mobility. In particular, the mass transfer of labour from the backward world to those regions where the growing international division of labour is enlarging high-wage job opportunities would have optimized the global location of factors and activities and narrowed the major disparities in incomes and standards of living.

This happy solution is ruled out by the political organization of the world in a system of nation-states. The inhabitants of any territory which is a focus of world economic growth have an interest in monopolizing its benefits; and they will accordingly exploit the apparatus of the state to restrict the access of others to the territory. Moreover, as affluence increases their technological and military capacity, they will deploy their increased power to subjugate other peoples for their own ends. The forms of subjugation may include direct colonial rule or combinations of political, economic, and military pressure on and inducement to foreign governments: the ends would be a transfer of income to the people of the dominant state in excess of what the free market process would ensure.

International inequalities are not therefore self-limiting—indeed they may widen cumulatively—and peaceful large-scale flows of labour across borders are far from normal phenomena. In a world of relative labour immobility, the development of backward regions has its own specific dynamics. Its main propellants are the various repercussions of growth in the advanced world which I have already studied: export expansion, military pressure, demonstration effects, and population explosion.

These forces have been analysed in detail earlier; but a word or two remains to be said about how the growth processes they stimulate fit into the pattern of international economic development.

First, I have suggested that the economies of scale achievable within the large domestic markets of the rich, densely populated countries give them a comparative advantage, in industrial exports. This advantage, however, is a function of the costs of transporting the products: with perfect mobility of goods, a local market is no less accessible to the foreign producer than to the local manufacturer; and, while this state of things remains a neo-classical fantasy, the differential advantage that scale factors give to manufacturers in rich countries certainly melts away as transport costs fall.

The effect is accentuated as the labour cost differential between rich and poor countries begins to count for more. This may happen as the wage differential widens to a degree where it simply outweighs all other considerations in industries with large requirements of low skilled labour. Further, lower labour costs may soon be translated into cheaper skills. The governments of poor countries—driven by the forces we have mentioned into a commitment to development—may begin subsidizing the learning process; and the impact of this on skilled labour costs—though diluted by the brain-drain—is sure to crode the competitive superiority of manufactures produced in rich countries.

Along with the purely economic dimensions of development in poor countries goes an increase in military capacity. Together these two factors would eventually undermine the ascendancy of the rich densely populated countries in the hierarchy of nations. They would also pave the way for the ultimate absorption of the backward world into the mainstream of international trade and development on a basis of relative equality.

The rich populous nations need not lose in absolute terms. Indeed, the development of the backward countries, by enlarging the world market, would open up further economies of scale—if the trading countries could develop a finer web of specialization. The rich, densely populated world can share in these benefits by specializing more narrowly than before. All the same, it will no longer be the focus of world economic growth.

The development of the world economy can thus be described in terms of a cycle with three phases: first, the concentration of growth impulses in a nuclear area, resulting in its intensive development; secondly, the rise of a new pattern of international specialization, as resource scarcities in the nuclear area compel it to rely increasingly on natural resourse-rich regions, resulting in the transmission of growth to the latter; and, finally, catching-up—through the advantage of cheap labour as well as through politically forced development—of the regions left out of this pattern of specialization. Meanwhile, some of the resource-rich regions may emerge as the new foci of the world economy—and the momentum of the cycle will be renewed.

The global balance of political power will sway in step with that of economic affluence, from the initial hegemony of the nuclear area, through a phase of shared dominance by it and the resource-rich regions, to an eventual eclipse of the nucleus and the rise to supremacy of the resource-rich regions along with new centres of power from among the areas earlier left behind.

The evolution of the world economy, since the era of ocean navigation, has followed this sequence closely. The unique suitability of western Europe, and particularly of Britain, as the springboard for exploration and control of the ocean trade routes produced the concentration of growth impulses there which sparked off the Industrial Revolution. The resulting pressure on natural resources led to the transmission of the growth impulse to resource-rich regions, particularly of the New World. The fruits of this new international division of labour, the accompanying development of land transport technology, and the economies of scale that all this generated helped renew the momentum of western European growth. Yet western Europe—and especially Britain— inexorably lost its economic and political leadership in world affairs. Meanwhile, development accelerated in the countries that had trailed behind in the earlier phases of the Industrial Revolution, giving rise to the present international power structure. All these processes will be described in fuller detail later and need no elaboration here.

An Example: The Rise and Fall of the Roman World

An example from an altogether different historical epoch relates to the rise and fall of the Roman empire. The economic and political development of the classical world is, of course, a familiar story.

The growth of population and income in the Greek city states created pressures on their limited arable area and thin, rocky soils, forcing them to depend increasingly on colonization and trade. The trade pattern consisted primarily of the exchange of the wine, oil, and manufactures of Greece for food from Sicily, Egypt, and the Black Sea coasts. But trade expansion was not compatible with the city-state form of political organization. The interminable struggle for trade and colonies between rival cities precipitated the Peloponnesian War and its sequel—a state of political and economic anarchy suddenly resolved by the rise of the Macedonian Empire spanning the eastern Mediterranean and the Middle East. Unfortunately, Alexander's empire could not survive the problems of communication overland with its far-flung marches. The most rapid and efficient mode of long-distance transport was navigation in landlocked waters; and the entire Mediterranean basin constituted in this age an area for trade expansion which was more logical than the Macedonian endeavour to link up the silk road and the caravan routes of Persia with Aegean commerce. Crucial to a Mediterranean-wide trading network was the link between the eastern and western Mediterranean through the Straits of Messina and the sea-corridor between the African coast and Sicily. Italy, because of her control of this major crossroads of Mediterranean traffic, was potentially the dominant power of the Mediterranean world; and Rome in turn, from her mathematically central position in Italy, could dominate the peninsula. After the decisive struggle for supremacy in the Mediterranean between Rome and her rival Carthage (located significantly on the Tunisian coast just across from Sicily), Rome became the focus of the expansionary forces of the classical world. Her central position made her not only the commercial hub of the Mediterranean but also its strategic pivot. It fell to her, therefore, to export the military and political services that sustained the Pax Romana which was the basis of the expansion of Mediterranean trade. A new international division of labour evolved, in which she relied increasingly on imports, particularly of food, from the far-flung provinces of her Empire.

As the development of the provinces—of Gaul, of Spain, of Egypt—was thus stimulated, the provincial markets for plantation products and manufactures expanded. Given the climatic homogeneity of the Mediterranean basin, it became worthwhile for the provinces to produce their own oil and wine and manufactures. A steady outflow of capital and skilled craftsmen from Rome to the provinces was induced; and whatever export advantages the metropolis may have commanded in respect of purely economic goods and services melted away.

The fiscal consequences of this were twofold. First the dispersal of production and taxable capacity from the capital to the provinces increased the cost of tax collection and the resistance it encountered, Secondly, the deterioration in Rome's terms of trade, the rising prices of her imports, eroded the real value of her tax receipts and increased her revenue requirements. The later Empire was a picture of chronic financial crisis—of a continuous drain of gold to the eastern Mediterranean and beyond the frontiers of the Empire, of inflation and—especially from the reign of Marcus Aurelius—of rapid deterioration of the currency. The attempts of Diocletian and Constantine to restore fiscal order and stabilize prices were ineffectual except in the East (for reasons we shall shortly discuss), but their effort to preserve the existing industrial structure as a living fossil by attaching labourers hereditarily to their current employments is most revealing.

The military and financial problems of Rome were multiplied manifold by the repercussions of the Empire on the barbarians beyond its pale. Largely excluded from the benefits of the Mediterranean trade but envious of the prosperity of the Empire, the barbarians exerted continuous military pressure on its frontiers. As the Empire expanded northwards, beyond the reaches of Mediterranean navigation, its supply lines became increasingly attenuated because of the backwardness of land transport (despite the best efforts of the Roman road-builders); and the defence of the northern perimeter absorbed an ever-larger proportion of imperial resources. Defence costs mounted all the more rapidly as the barbarians increased their military capacity by their peripheral trade with the Empire and by assimilation of the technological lessons it provided.

It was this combination of the pressure of what Toynbee (60) describes as the external proletariat and a contracting economic and fiscal base that undermined the authority of Rome. With Rome an economic deadweight, the western Empire crumbled and with it the commercial economies of Gaul, Spain, Northern Italy, and Africa. The eastern Mediterranean, however, withstood the crisis. For, while the West was the end of the then-known world, the East was

the gateway to the Orient, the link with the vast spaces and populations, the fabulous wealth and exotic resources of Asia. Thus,
western trade was a local affair and declined with the increasing
self-sufficiency of its regional units. But eastern commerce was
intercontinental: the current of trade through Constantinople and
the Levant was stronger and fluctuated but little with local disturb-
ances. More importantly, the East had—in Egypt in particular, but
also in coastal Syria and Asia Minor—exceptionally fertile provinces with good water communication, and geographic immunity
from barbarian invasion, which constituted an enduring fiscal base.
The western provinces—Italy, Gaul, even Spain—did not enjoy
comparable security, and possibly not comparable fertility or
accessibility. Constantinople, therefore, inherited the Empire; but
it was too remote to control the western Mediterranean and,though
Justinian briefly restored the unity of the entire Mediterranean
basin, this proved but a passing episode in the long descent of the
West into the depths of feudalism.

The Prime Movers of World Growth

I have examined how growth processes are sustained and transmitted from one part of the world economy to another. But what are
the forces that might initiate growth if the international system is
stagnant to begin with? What are the equivalents on the global
plane of the factors we have described as the prime movers of
national economic development?

I suggest that there are essentially two: population pressure, and
military competition. The conservative social processes of taste-
formation imply that a stagnant society does not generate wants it
cannot fulfil. If a closed system—like the world economy—
stagnates, consumption demands per head are not likely to change,
and growth processes originating in this factor are virtually ruled
out. But while specific tastes are socially formed—both in their
qualitative and quantitative aspects—self-preservation is a primary
instinct. It is little modified by social learning and forms, as such,
the irreducible basis for progress even amidst general social stagnation. Both our prime movers of growth derive from this instinct for
survival.

The urge to prolong life as much as possible motivates an endless
search for ways to reduce the death rate. It also leads to efforts to
conserve any random increase in numbers. Population, therefore,

has a natural buoyancy which stagnant societies typically control through practices like abortion, infanticide, delayed marriage, prolonged lactation, and contraception. But these controls are rather precarious; for most societies are not homogeneous, but embody a variety of traditions and beliefs—including value systems (like the major world religions)—which foster fertility by disapproving of abortion, infanticide, sometimes contraception, homosexuality, incest, masturbation, and anything else that might deflect the sexual instinct from its normal reproductive outlet. If there is any room for population growth, groups subscribing to such values would therefore, ultimately dominate society. The fruitful may inherit the earth; indeed, that perhaps is the reason why so many of the major religions urge the faithful to multiply. Population in any complex society is therefore driven repeatedly against its Malthusian limit—even though the frequency of collision may be reduced by the devices I have mentioned.

The military factor, no less than the demographic, answers the need for self-preservation. Given man's predatory ways, self-defence is an imperative for survival. The direct and indirect consequences of war are among the greatest of all causes of death. Yet effective defence requires military-technological parity with the foe; and the fear of being left behind, of yielding a temporary, but possibly lethal, advantage to one's enemies stimulates societies to unremitting effort in improving their military potential. This is so even in a stagnant world. Indeed, it may be all the more so in the midst of general stagnation—since here one's loss is the other's gain, and the interactions between societies assume therefore a zero-sum, directly antagonistic character.

Military competition and population pressure, then, will inevitably emerge even in the most profound depths of general stagnation—and revival is accordingly assured. Thus it is that the mainstream of global economic growth has never been permanently damned: with time it has burst through the most insuperable of technological barriers—and the current of human evolution has thereby been sustained.

Part Two

I have so far been attempting to fashion some kind of a general framework within which historical growth processes can be interpreted as adaptations to a specific set of environmental opportunities and pressures. In what follows, I try to apply this framework to the modern economic history of a few selected countries.

I begin with the seminal example of Britain—the prototype of development essentially through the market in response to export opportunity; I touch on the political and military correlates of such a process.

This is followed by a delineation of a broad class of economies in which development through the market is aborted—where vigorous intervention by the state in the economy is an imperative of growth. Manchu China is studied as an example. I examine in particular the factors that accounted for the absence of a positive development policy. What was it that made the imperial system so impervious to the pressures for development; and, how did these pressures—unable to bend the Empire—ultimately break it? A logical sequel to these questions is an analysis of the effect of these pressures on the character and economic pattern of the new order in China.

India belongs to the same family of economies in which market-induced development fails and the state is required to play an active role in any growth process. However, she is subject to a different constellation of pressures for development. In consequence, the pattern of her development policies diverges very sharply from the Chinese.

The Russian model is closer to the Chinese—in motive forces and general economic pattern—though some historical differences in the nature of military pressure on the two economies can be invoked to explain their dissimilarity.

Like India, Russia, and China, Tokugawa Japan belonged to the class of densely-populated poor countries, but the lesser durability of her political institutions than those of the Manchu (due ultimately to geographic differences) proved for Japan a decisive advantage. This was coupled with windfall successes for Japanese exports—so that the Japanese experience lies midway between the two polar models we have sketched—the British and the Chinese. These three cases—the Indian, the Russian, and the Japanese—are touched briefly essentially in the context of comparison with the Chinese.

A final chapter tries again to restore the global perspective. It is an analysis of the history and causes of international income inequality looked at from the point of view of the world system as a whole.

7

EXPORTS AND DEVELOPMENT THROUGH
THE MARKET: THE RISE AND FALL
OF BRITAIN

THE first Industrial Revolution has often been regarded as the prototype of all Industrial Revolutions. In our taxonomy, however, British economic growth figures essentially as the classic example of export-propelled development. The growth of the British economy over the ages was, of course, neither rapid nor smooth. It spanned many centuries from the time of the Tudors: and it was imperilled so severely by institutional and natural resource constraints that, but for the fact that the stimulus of her export potential was maintained throughout, it would surely have flickered out without fuelling a sequence of revolutions in politics and technology as it eventually did.

Some recent historians have doubted whether the Industrial Revolution of the late eighteenth century was indeed export-led. Deane and Cole (13) and Hartwell (24), for instance, argue that the spectacular late eighteenth-century expansion of exports—especially of the most rapidly growing manufactures—flowed mainly to dependent colonial economies in America and the West Indies, whose demand and income derived essentially from their exports to the metropolis. Britain's export growth—in this scheme—was not an autonomous propellant but a derivative of the growth of the domestic economy. Others assert that this is an inaccurate picture of a process of expansion through trade and division of labour within the unified Atlantic economy (Davis (11, 12), Berrill (3)).

I need not enter the tangled thicket of this controversy, since I am not concerned with the causation of the eighteenth-century Industrial Revolution as such. Indeed, substantial domestic British expansion before the late eighteenth century is integral to my analysis. The Industrial Revolution is, for me, the culmination of a long process of slow growth and associated political change dating back to the new sea routes of the Tudor era. I argue that the new geography of ocean navigation was an essentially autonomous bounty for Britain, that it stimulated export (of goods and—especially—of services) and the growth of empire and a resulting slow but—from the early eighteenth century—steady domestic expansion, and that the geographical uniqueness of Britain was such that this stimulus was stronger and lasted longer in England than in any of her rivals—long enough indeed for the resulting expansion process to induce the political and technological innovations that led up to the Industrial Revolution.

Location and Military-Commercial Advantage

The key to England's development since the sixteenth century is its location. In the era of ocean navigation after Vasco da Gama and Columbus, an island just off the Atlantic coast of Europe, controlling access from the ocean to the Baltic, the Rhine, and the northern shores of France was at a unique positional advantage. As a principal node in the world transport network, it was bound to become a major crossroads of trade. Geopolitically it enjoyed a certain security from invasion; at the same time, it was in a position to intercept much of the booming Atlantic trade of north-west Europe. It was potentially the major exporter of shipping and trading services—and also of the ancillary facilities of international banking and insurance which are so closely connected with trade.

None of England's rivals were quite as favoured by geography. Spain and Portugal, though Atlantic economies themselves, had as their natural hinterland the contracting Mediterranean world rather than the flourishing Atlantic sea-board. France—apart from the provinces of Brittany and Normandy—was too continental and agricultural to develop a comparative advantage in maritime trade. So was Germany.

Of the European powers, Holland alone could have matched England's maritime potential, and did so until its fatal positional weakness was exposed and exploited by the English Navigation Acts of 1651 and later. These required that all English imports be carried either in English ships or in ships belonging to the country of origin and that all colonial trade be carried in English ships alone. The acts were aimed at the Dutch shipping and entrepôt business. They provoked the Anglo–Dutch wars in which England's geopolitical advantage—her position squarely across the main ocean routes to north and north-west Europe—proved decisive. England bestraddled the lifeline of Dutch commerce: in the war of 1652–4 alone, she captured 1700 Dutch prizes and undermined the naval aspirations and commercial potential of Holland for ever.

Two other geopolitical factors contributed to the issue of the Anglo-Dutch struggle: Holland's land frontier, the defence of which diverted resources from the all-important navy; and her shallow estuarine harbours, which could accommodate only lightly-armed, flat-bottomed ships in contrast to the heavily-armed, deep-draught men-o'-war based on England's deep-water ports.

All this is not to suggest that the Dutch economy fell into a precipitous decline after the Anglo-Dutch wars. The legacy of the past survived in some measure: most, if not all, the colonial posses-sions remained intact; the trading connections endured, as did the vast stocks of commercial and sea-faring lore and mercantile capital. But the Dutch share in the growth of world trade fell off sharply; colonial expansion was arrested; with the loss of their naval ascendancy, the Dutch could no longer control access even to their once-impregnable commercial strongholds in the Baltic and central Europe, so that the West could increasingly bypass Amsterdam and trade with Germany and the Baltic either directly or through Hamburg. Holland's decline from the closing decades of her Golden Century was in growth rates (rather than absolute levels), in investment opportunities, and in interest rates—as the Dutch abdi-cated their entrepreneurial functions in world trade for the role of rentier-financiers. Above all, as defence costs and the consequent taxation of necessities mounted, the wage rate was driven up and the competitive position of Dutch industry eroded—beginning with the labour-intensive industries but extending rapidly to the whole range of manufactures (Wilson (63, 64,65)).

England's commercial supremacy both preceded her industrial ascendancy and outlasted it. It began in the late seventeenth century after the Navigation Acts and the Dutch Wars and persisted till the 1920's—quite fifty years after the loss of her industrial leadership.

Associated with commerce, too, was empire. In part, the Empire was directly a function of trade, designed to ensure monopolistic control of England's supply sources and markets. In part, however, it was a corollary of her mastery of the sea and the temptation to cash in on this wherever a power vacuum existed ashore.

In the age of ocean transport, then, the logic of location was the prime mover behind England's development—whether it worked through mercantile income, buccaneering booty, or imperial tribute. It was a force which was sustained over centuries—from the sixteenth to the late nineteenth. Only in the age of the railroad and the automobile—when overland trade and transport at last eclipsed overseas commerce—was its momentum finally spent.

Commercial Expansion and the Revolution of the Seventeenth Century

In the sixteenth and early seventeenth centuries, the repercussions of ocean navigation were narrowly circumscribed by the regulatory apparatus of the government. The system of licences and charters of monopoly enmeshed virtually all industry and trade. In long-distance ocean trade in its pioneering days, a charter of monopoly had an essential economic function: by protecting the profits on pioneering investment, it internalized the external economies in terms of new knowledge that such investment generated. But once such knowledge had been acquired, the monopoly became a fetter on progress. This was even more so in the extensive sphere of industry where no major innovations were immediately necessary. Here the consequences of monopoly-by-fiat were restrictive on two counts: first, through the direct restriction of output; second, through its distributional bias in favour of the small circle of privileged businessmen, courtiers, and the king, and against consumers and producers at large. Given the income distribution effects of monopoly, growth benefited primarily the few rich—whose affluence overflowed into the small-scale luxury crafts and not into the mass-production industries at all.

Even though thus restricted, the expansionary effects of ocean navigation were too much for the inelastic natural resource base of Elizabethan England. The initial consequences were an intense demand for food, wool, and timber. Food was needed to support the increasing numbers that prosperity made possible, wool to supply the expanding export both of the primary product and of the textile. Timber requirements were more complex. There was first, the demand for building timber and domestic and industrial fuel created by population growth; second, the demand of the expanding ship-building industry, and third, the need for wood for charcoal-smelting in an age when metallurgy was booming under the impetus of war and plunder along the new trade routes.

The rising demand for food and wood led to deforestation and increasing pressure on the land. The pressure on the land was the more severe because of social restrictions on land use—the legal bars on the conversion of arable to pasture, the common grazing rights, and the hunting rights of the king and his greater subjects.

The combined restrictiveness of policy and resources precipitated the crisis of the seventeenth century. From the 1620s, there was a pause in population growth, a reversal of industrial progress, and a consequent intensification of social conflicts. The seventeenth century nurtured revolution as no other period in English history.

The environment for revolution was created by expanding export opportunity which enriched a few monopolists while stirring the emulation of the many. A demonstration effect was produced on large groups of merchants and squires—but the aspirations thus fired were frustrated by the restrictiveness of the old order. Hence, the long turmoil of the Stuart era.

In the aftermath of revolution, the monarchy and the peerage were reduced to narrowly-defined constitutional roles while power gravitated through parliament to the gentry—the new Whig oligarchy of capitalist farmers and their industrial and mercantile allies.

Under the new dispensation, the structure of monopoly privilege was rapidly dismantled. The forest rights of the crown and the peerage were curtailed and the enclosure movement acquired a new momentum. Freedom of competition and land use were increasingly assured. Foreign policy, meanwhile, came to mirror the mercantile interest as never before. The Navigation Acts, control of the seas, a far-flung Empire acquired not in a fit of absent-mindedness but in the very conscious pursuit of profit—all fitted into a policy designed to make England the commercial metropolis of the western World.

An age when ocean navigation was being revolutionized had its own political characteristics. The sea was becoming a world-wide domain, a unified trading area which required policing and invited imperial control: given the economies of scale in the exercise of coercive authority and the falling costs of maritime transport, the stage was set for a monopolistic domination of the oceans. And in the struggle for the mastery of the seas, Britain's geopolitical uniqueness stood her in good stead. She became the political and economic focus of a world-wide economy and empire, just as Rome had been the centre of the Mediterranean world in the era when navigation was confined to landlocked waters.

Export-induced Growth and Innovation
Thus the way was paved for the Commercial Revolution. A flood of
earnings from shipping, commercial services, and imperial tribute
(payment perhaps for political services!) swelled domestic demand.

Some points about the growth of the domestic market need
emphasizing. Since England was a relatively advanced economy,
English industries had but few large-scale foreign competitors to
confront; thus a rather modest expansion of the home market was
enough to render most of them viable. This also implied that the
initial capital requirements of most industries were small; hence,
control of new industrial and mercantile wealth was widely diffused,
the prospering classes comprising not a negligible handful but a
substantial middle class which constituted a homogeneous mass
market for standardized goods. Market-oriented industries were
thus stimulated, while England's entrepôt situation—which made
her the junction point of routes from many material sources and to
many markets—attracted other kinds of production.

The pressure on England's resource base that resulted from all
this expansion had two dimensions—agricultural and mineral. In
agriculture, the political changes of the seventeenth century had
prepared the way for a technological revolution. The innovations of
the late seventeenth and early eighteenth centuries resolved—
temporarily at least—England's food problems. But in mining the
shortages formed an interrelated network. Industrialization required increasing inputs: iron (for fast-working and durable
machinery) and coal (for fuel). But in an age of charcoal-smelting,
deforestation had left iron supplies dependent on expensive imports
from Sweden. Coal production, too, was restricted by problems of
drainage as mines were deepened. The innovations that resolved
these inelasticities—coke-smelting of iron-ore, and the steam
engine—formed a closely linked cluster. Steam engines not only
pumped water out of mines, but also powered hot blasts through
furnaces and coke ovens. Coke-smelting multiplied the demand for
coal. Steam engines themselves were to become—as industrialization progressed—a vast source of demand for both coal and iron.
Together, the coal–iron–steam complex constituted a radical
technological transformation, substituting an abundant domestic
resource for one increasingly scarce at home and abroad. It was a
substitution which was completed only with the improvements and
economies of the late eighteenth century—Watt's condenser and

Cort's puddling process. However, Darby's and Newcomen's inventions had resolved the most critical bottlenecks early in the eighteenth century. Over the hundred years that followed the Restoration, the growth process gathered momentum—though interrupted by the harvest failures of the early eighteenth century.

The really revolutionary industry of eighteenth-century England—the one on which revolutionary interpretations of British economic growth focus—was cotton textiles. Indeed, traditional chronology, from Toynbee to Hobsbawm, dates the Idustrial Revolution from the cluster of innovations in cotton spinning abut 1760 and the spectacular expansion in textile output that accompanied it. Textiles, of course, are the most basic of necessities next only to food. They commanded as such a vast market even at relatively low levels of development. And, given the possibilities of substitution for other fibres, the demand for cotton textiles in particular was almost infinitely elastic. This was all the more so for the products of a country which—by virtue of its location and its Empire—enjoyed such easy access to continental and colonial markets.

The supply of raw material from the New World was as elastic as the demand for cotton textiles. A vast sales potential thus awaited the innovator who could reduce the prime cost of cotton textile production by increasing labour productivity. The innovational response was not as abrupt as it is usually made out to be. Certainly, it was phased. Kay's flying shuttle (1738) multiplied labour productivity in weaving manifold; but more than two decades passed before the diffusion of Kay's invention and the resulting spurt in demand for yarn went far enough to stimulate changes in spinning technology. Thereafter, of course, all constraints on the industry disappeared and its astronomical expansion was assured.

But, despite the drama of the expansion of cotton textiles, the British economy as a whole grew not in a sudden dramatic burst but by slow and sustained acceleration. It is doubtful if any sharp discontinuities could be discerned in any of the aggregative time series. The cotton textile industry had relatively small technical linkages with the rest of the economy—despite its demand for textile machinery and steam engines, for bleaching, dyeing, and finishing services. And, of course, as we have seen, the mushrooming of the textile industry itself could be traced back to long-run evolutionary factors.

The growth of industry in nineteenth-century England was much accelerated by economies of scale. These were factors, both internal and external to the firm and the industry, which—as the industrial economy grew—not only made England an attractive location for more manufactures, but also increased the productivity of inputs, the rate of profit, and the incentive to reinvest. In the English case, the scale effects were accentuated by the high degree of localization of the minerals on which the Industrial Revolution was based. With coal and iron occurring in close proximity, England tended to develop industrial belts where intense concentration of population and industry made economies of scale easily accessible to manufacturers.

Resource Scarcities and the Climacteric and Decline

The rise of cotton, coal, and iron, the accompanying urban-industrial boom, and the demographic revolution generated pressures at two main points of the early nineteenth-century British economy. The first was inland transport. As the factory system expanded, the canal network, developed in response to the smaller demands of the eighteenth century, could no longer cope with the need for rapid movement of growing masses of materials and products. The resulting shortages led to the invention of the railway, which resolved on a long-term basis the problem of internal mobility.

A much more intractable problem was that of food supply. The nineteenth-century explosion of population and income accelerated the growth of demand. There was a respite from scarcity following the Napoleonic wars, when the marginal acreage converted to wheat because of high wartime prices acted as a cushion. But, by 1835, this excess capacity had been absorbed, and the momentum of rising demand began to outstrip the growth potential of British agricultue. Steep rises in cereal prices seemed imminent—with resulting erosion of real wages, intensification of class tensions, and Malthusian-Ricardian stresses on the rate of growth. However, the crisis precipitated its own solution. In 1846, the Corn Laws were abolished and Britain opened up to food imports. In the short run, acute food-price inflation was averted through imports from Europe. In the long run, agricultural development in the continental interiors of the New World was stimulated, and a new pattern of international specialization began to unfold.

The resulting spectacular growth in the volume of traffic induced a technological revolution in transport, oceanic as well as continental. The margins between delivery prices and costs of production fell steeply from the 1870s, food and raw material prices in Europe plunged under the impact of the deluge from America, accelerating the rise in real wages and popular standards of living.

Yet, for Britain's long-run economic ascendancy, the consequences were not merely momentous but fateful. The expansion of Britain's primary imports was the driving force behind the settlement and development of the New World; that new invention—the railway—was the vehicle of the process. Through this channel, the expansionary impulses of industrial Britain overflowed abroad. In America, the rising flood of export income supported a buoyant home market in which American manufacturers could enjoy increasing economies of scale. The result was to erode the competitive position of British industrial products first in American markets, then in third countries, and eventually in Britain itself. Meanwhile, the high returns on investment in the New World began to draw capital away from Britain.

As England's industrial leadership was undermined, the economies of scale factor began to work in favour of the United States and Germany with their now larger industrial markets and thus to accelerate the decline of England. The relative eclipse of British manufactures came first, but it was followed by loss of leadership in shipping and commerce and finally in money and banking.

In a wider perspective, the economic decline of Britain can be seen as part of an inexorable global process. For two hundred years up to the late nineteenth century, the oceans were the main highways of long-distance transport: economic development everywhere was essentially littoral in character with maritime countries and areas exercising a dominant influence on the affairs of the world. The main trade networks spanned oceans rather than continents, linking distant lands in a cosmopolitan economy which formed the basis of the colonial system.

Since then, for reasons which I have already explained, the major technical problems of communication over land have been solved. The interiors of great land masses have been penetrated, explored, and finally unified by the railroad, the motorized highway, and the aeroplane. No such dramatic acceleration has occurred in ocean navigation. The profitability of inland commerce, therefore, has increased far faster than that of overseas trade—especially the long-distance trade between the developed and the underdevel-

oped worlds—which has accordingly dwindled in relative importance. On the political level, the old imperial order has receded. The
Pax Britannica has been replaced by the global economic and
political dominance of the great continental powers. In the new
world of the twentieth century, the economic basis of the old British
way of life has disappeared leaving for the former masters of the
globe a future of genteel decay.

8

THE FAILURE OF THE MARKET IN DENSELY
POPULATED BACKWARD SOCIETIES

AFTER the British example of the dynamics of market-induced growth we turn to the analysis of economies where the market is incapable of sustaining the development process. A theoretical exercise is, however, the necessary prelude to actual case study. One must explain why the market failed to accomplish in one group of countries what it so successfully achieved in others. In this chapter, I assume the functioning of a free market, constrained only by the international immobility of labour. I design, on this premiss, a model of stagnation in one broad class of economies—the poor and populous ones. In the process, some traditional theories of backwardness are discarded, and an interesting sidelight is thrown on some of the darker corridors of international trade theory.

The Vicious Circle and the Capacity to Save

Scarcity of capital and low rates of accumulation are universal characteristics of backward economies. Economists like Nurkse (43) and Rostow (53) regard them virtually as the criteria of backwardness. Indeed the most popular explanation of backwardness in the folklore of development is that backward economies are prisoners within a vicious circle of poverty and low capacity to save and invest: they are too poor to improve their lot by accumulation— so they remain poor for ever.

Apart from the mystery of how such economies can ever develop on their own—as they are sometimes seen to do—there are at least two flaws in this story. First, there are the facts of income distribution. In such economies, particularly the densely-populated ones, much of the total income—far more, in fact, than in the developed world—goes to the few rich for whom capacity to save is no constraint whatsoever: yet the outcome is not a high rate of investment but a perennial orgy of conspicuous consumption.

This paradox has always attracted sociologists like a magnet. Backward people—the sociologists have told us—are not just poor but peculiar: their élites in particular are peculiar in that they prefer status to achievement and are more interested, therefore, in displaying what they have to impress the onlooker than in adding to it. The sociological model of backwardness has been embraced by a whole tribe of economists with understandable glee: here, they feel, is the *deus ex machina* that will spare them a painful search for an economic explanation of the paradoxical facts. But will it really? Doesn't the sociological explanation raise at least as many questions as it answers? Why, for instance, do élites in backward countries cherish their supposedly peculiar values? Do their preferences reflect economic conditions? Or are they purely a product of the cultural environment? Is culture in turn autonomous or is it primarily an adaptation to economic necessities? In fact Pandora's box is opened up and the economist may find it safer to retreat from the allurements of sociology to drearier but more familiar territory.

Such a retreat becomes all the more necessary when one considers the other break in the supposedly vicious circle. This break is the result of international capital mobility. An economy which does not generate much saving domestically may yet attract enough foreign capital for rapid growth. This has happened often enough in the past. One need only recall the migration of Dutch, Flemish, and Huguenot capital into seventeenth-century England or the mass exodus of British capital to the New World in the latter half of the nineteenth century. Yet many backward countries have remained backward after long periods in which political conditions were ideal for capital inflow. Indeed, the picture is typically one of large-scale capital outflow—so that the limit supposedly set to growth by domestic savings is never reached.

Returns to Capital and Neo-Classical Trade Theory

Clearly, the incentive to invest is a far more effective constraint. And here lies a puzzle for international trade theorists as well as development economists, since the inadequacy of investment incentives in capital-poor economies directly contradicts the factor-proportions theory of international trade. A simple two-factor neo-classical model in which a capital-rich economy trades with a labour-rich one would either equalize factor prices or, if factor endowments in the two countries do not lie within the same 'equalization zone', leave the labour-rich economy with lower wages and a higher rate of return to capital. Wages, of course, are lower in the backward countries of the real world. But not a shred of evidence exists to suggest that the return on capital (and therefore the inducement to invest) is higher. Neither a direct comparison of profit rates nor the indirect evidence of private capital flows would bear this out. How did the neo-classical model go so far wrong?

The answer lies in the neo-classical assumptions of perfect mobility of goods and competitive equilibrium under constant returns to scale. These together imply that profit rates are independent of local differences in intensities of demand. In fact, of course, transport costs are very positive indeed and economies of scale are so pervasive in manufacturing industry as to make of perfect competition a mere myth.

The cost level of an industry then has at least two components: first, processing costs, which—given the production function—depend both on the scale of output and on factor prices; and secondly, distribution costs, which depend on transport rates and the spatial density of demand.

Low wages reduce processing costs, for any given output, to an extent determined by the labour-intensity of production. Proximity to a large market, on the other hand, is a distributional advantage which is proportional to the level of freight rates. The relative significance of processing and distributional factors depends on the price-elasticity of demand: the more elastic the market the easier it would be to translate a processing advantage into larger sales within a given area, and the less accordingly would be the necessity of exploring distant markets at higher distribution costs. In the real world of transport costs and economies of scale, then, both the volume and the elasticity of domestic demand affect the rate of profit; and their effect may oppose and indeed swamp that of labour costs.

Of course, in industries and at times of very low freights, wages do count rather more as a determinant of profit rates. Even in such circumstances, however, there are precious few industries in which cheap unskilled labour is crucial. Cheap mechanical skills matter very much more. But the growth of industrial skills—where it is not a function of capital investment—depends on industrial experience; it is an economy of scale—whether external Marshallian (40) or internal Arrovian (1). To spell this point out: industrial skills are relatively abundant in advanced countries. In the backward world, however, their development is retarded by two factors. First, skill-formation implies a learning process of which the trainee is the ultimate beneficiary. The cost of training, however, is too high for the trainee to bear out of current income in a low-wage economy; it must be borne largely by someone else. But, since labour is not appropriable except under slavery, the investor in the learning process may be unable to recover his investment; it will at best have the character of an unsecured loan. This consideration inevitably restricts investment in skill-formation. A second consideration arises out of economies of scale in the production of skills. The existence of cheap training facilities requires the existence of a large market for the skill in question. In this, as in all increasing returns phenomena, a large domestic market confers a decisive advantage.

Now in the backward country's markets, the demand for income-elastic products is restricted both by the very low *per capita* income and by the extreme skewness of the income distribution. Both these characteristics follow in turn from the factor endowment. That the intense population pressure on other factors would lead to low *per capita* income is obvious. That it also polarizes the income distribution sharply has been explained in an earlier chapter.

In such an economy, the mass of the very poor cannot afford any but the most elementary necessities. The microscopic élite, on the other hand, is too small to constitute a large market for any one good: it demands a wide variety of products, each in small quantities. The market for each manufacture is not just narrow but inelastic: in the absence of a middle class, moderate price cuts do not make the product accessible to very many more consumers than before. All this has two implications. First, in industries where economies of scale are very substantial, local manufacturers are ousted by rivals based on the mass markets of developed countries. Secondly, even in industries where transport costs and tariffs offer adequate protection, the number of local producers is small. Now an oligopolist in a narrow and inelastic market can increase his sales only by slashing prices drastically—especially since his rivals may be expected to match any price cut. His marginal revenue function is both low and steep.

A low and inelastic curve of the marginal revenue product of industrial investment follows. The low level of the curve means little investment in manufacturing; its inelasticity implies that an increased capacity to save—reflected in a lower interest rate—may not notably accelerate accumulation in this sector unless the market expands.

A New View of Trade and Investment

Put all this back in the frame of an international system in which labour is immobile between countries while capital is not. In such a system, manufacturing industries are attracted by economies of scale to zones where high income-earners cluster, agricultural investment to regions with high land/labour ratios. Exchange between these areas constitutes the mainstream of international trade. The poor densely-populated regions, on the othr hand, lack comparative advantage in anything very much in a world where labour services are non-tradeable. The exceptions would be the very few manufactures in which economies of scale are sufficient to swamp low wage costs. Of these, the cotton textile industry is perhaps the most important current example. It is, of course, precisely in such labour-intensive industries that labour organization is most strongly entrenched in the mature economies. The pressure of this vocal interest group leads to severe restriction of labour-intensive imports. Hence the export potential of the underdeveloped countries in labour-intensive manufactures remains as unfulfilled as in labour services. They therefore participate but marginally in world trade. Being thus essentially self-sufficient, their production pattern reflects their demand pattern. It is dominated by food production along with some labour-intensive small-scale manufactures either of elementary necessities like coarse cloth or of luxury handicrafts and an extensive tertiary sector of unskilled services. All these sectors survive the potential competition of imports through extremely low wage levels.

This is not to deny that a poor overcrowded economy may sometimes capitalize on a unique geographical endowment to develop a specific export staple—indigo or opium, tea or jute, cotton or sugar or tin. But generally this can promise only marginal relief to a zone of intense population pressure on natural resources: here the reservoir of unexploited natural resource possibilities will lack the breadth and variety needed to make a substantial impact on the economy.

There are exceptions, of course. A twist of fate, a new technological departure, and the world may grow suddenly clamorous for the services of a resource controlled by the backward economy—so much indeed that its eventual expansion is virtually assured. Think of the effect of the discovery of the Atlantic trade routes on the demand for the shipping and trading services which Britain was so uniquely located to provide. Or consider the role of oil in the development of the Middle East today. About all this, there is an irreducible element of blind chance. One may well anticipate the problems that give rise to an innovation; but it would be impossible—almost by definition—to foresee its wider economic consequences. Given this state of ignorance, however, one may accept the admittedly crude generalization that the overall natural resource potential per head of an economy is related to its land area per head and that high population densities impose a corresponding disadvantage.

Further, it is not just a matter of a limited export potential. The scarcity of property resources relative to labour also results in an inequitable distribution of export income, so that, in terms of our familiar argument, its multiplier effects on the domestic market are small. Most of it flows back abroad in consumption imports or profit repatriation; the rest is reinvested in the export sector. This is the classic model of the dualistic plantation economy. Up to a point, the plantations grow—but they achieve only a tenuous link with the backward economy and remain essentially satellites of the advanced cosmopolitan system which they supply.

To sum up, in a backward densely-populated economy, industrial investment opportunities are limited by the domestic market, while investment outlets in the primary sector are restricted by the adverse man/land ratios. Market size is a limit not only to investment but also to innovation. Obviously, technical progress—to the extent that it is embodied in capital goods—is a function of gross investment. But, even if capital were perfectly malleable, innovation would be linked to market expansion by two factors. First, major technical progress is often localized at larger scales of production: it involves higher fixed commitments as the price of lower variable costs, so that unit costs fall only for larger scales of output. A plausible reason for this is that, over a period of relatively smaller-scale production, the scope for small-scale improvements will have been fully explored; hence the possibilities of further technical progress would be richer at the other end of the spectrum. Secondly, the incentive to research increases with the size of the market since the fixed costs of making a given invention can be spread over a larger output. On both these counts, stagnant markets drastically limit the search for and the adoption of new methods of production in the industrial sector of our backward economy. In the primary sector, the inelasticities of domestic supply are indeed more pressing than the market constraints. But they are offset by elastic supplies from abroad—from countries better endowed with natural resources—so that there is no excess demand to act as a sustained stimulus for innovation.

The Model and the Facts

This is a model of backwardness of considerable explanatory power. While focusing on the low rate of total capital formation, it explains also the small volume of foreign private investment and its orientation to primary exports. It accounts for the enclave character of the export sector—its failure either to expand enough to engulf the economy or to stimulate diversified growth. It sheds light on the limited role of such economies in world trade. It illuminates their industrial structure—the dominance of luxury handicrafts, elementary food processing, and textiles. Finally, it accounts for the expenditure pattern of the rich: it explains why, instead of investing in production, they waste their substance in riotous living, or on land, idle hoards, and jewellery, or even in investment abroad in foreign currency or equities. And all this without invoking the aid of the omniscient sociologist.

9

THE EXAMPLE OF CHINA

I Stagnation and Revolution under Empire and Republic

To the economic historian, the transition to modern economic development in China abounds in mysteries as deep as the ways of the supposedly inscrutable Orient. The Middle Kingdom of the Southern Sung was technologically the most sophisticated in the medieval world. It was the origin—long before their assimilation by Europe—of such crucial and diverse innovations as printing and gunpowder and firearms. It even developed techniques for the use of coal in iron-smelting—thus anticipating by six hundred years the innovation of Abraham Darby which paved the way for the Industrial Revolution in England. How then can one account for the immemorial stagnation that followed in the Ming and the Ch'ing, the six centuries of inertia that reduced the fabulous Cathay of Marco Polo to the backwardness of the nineteenth century? And what ended this long standstill? How in particular do the impact of the West and the rhythm of the classic dynastic cycle figure in the dynamics of modern Chinese history? If, as is often suggested, the transformation of China is a delayed response to the western intrusion, what explains the hundred-year lag?

In an earlier chapter, I have referred to China's modern economic history as a classic example of the operation of demographic and military pressures on a poor and populous economy. How in its details does the Chinese puzzle fit into my frame of reference?

The High-Level Equilibrium Trap and the Failure of the Market

The most interesting model of Chinese stagnation before the Communist Revolution is that of 'the high-level equilibrium trap'. This theory—articulated by Mark Elvin (17) and Dwight Perkins (47)—runs in terms of an exploding population exhausting opportunities for increase in output by absorption of unused natural resources, by intensification of traditional inputs, and indeed by innovation within the traditional technology. Agriculture evolved in the process into a sophisticated horticulture. Yields were so high

that the Communist government failed to improve them significantly until it switched to a reliance on modern industrial-scientific
inputs (chemical fertilizers and pesticides, power pumps, etc.) in
1961. Indeed, given the availability of new land—through the opening up of Manchuria in the twentieth century, for instance—
traditional agricultural technology was good enough to support an
industrial revolution such as happened in Manchuria in the 1930s.
Like agriculture, transport along the inland waterways was highly
developed. Land transport was not, essentially because the pervasiveness and efficiency of inland navigation rendered it super-
fluous. Despite the efficiency of traditional technology, the shor-
tage of food, of fibres, of fuels, of metals, of wood, of animals for
draught-power or farm-yard manure, above all of land—from
which all this was derived—drastically constricted growth. Population pressure on scarce natural resources had driven China to a
point of sharply diminishing, even negative, returns, progressively
eroding surpluses, rates of profit, and *per capita* incomes. Further
expansion required the bridging of major technological discontinuities, a great leap forward into the modern world of steam power,
electricity, and internal combustion engines, of chemical synthesis
and modern genetics—which internal forces could not possibly
generate.

There are, however, a few points about this model which need
emphasizing. First, the facts do not point to a negligible capacity to
save. Given the high levels of rent, of interest on consumption
lending, and returns on inventories, the potential surplus over
essential consumption (*à la* Baran) has been estimated by Carl
Riskin (51) as no less than 36 per cent of NDP in 1933. The critical
limit to growth was set, not by the rate of surplus, but by the rate of
profit as the determinant of the inducement to invest.

Secondly, while a closed economy may indeed grind to a halt
because of the Ricardian problem, additional assumptions would be
needed in an open economy to rule out the Ricardian solution. Why
couldn't China follow the path of England after the repeal of the
Corn Law? Why couldn't she have imported the primary products
she needed in exchange for manufactured exports? The answer
obviously is a matter of economies of scale and the size of the
domestic market. In all but the most elementary necessities, demand in China was small in volume and widely dispersed in spatial
pattern. Without mass markets and mass production, China could

never have matched the large-scale, low-cost industrial producers of advanced countries in international markets, despite her low wages. The one exception to this was the cotton textile industry. Here the Chinese market was indeed vast—but a distinction is essential, nevertheless, between the spinning and weaving sections of the industry. The distinction is relevant because of the almost free supply of idle labour that the discontinuous rhythm of agri-culture provided to rural handicrafts. This labour supply ensured the virtual immunity to factory competition of handicraft activity in some form or other. But handicraftsmen naturally concentrated on lines in which they enjoyed comparative advantage relative to the factory sector. In the textile industry, they specialized in weaving while absorbing yarn on a large scale from the mills. Modern producers, therefore—whether in China or abroad—could hardly penetrate the Chinese rural market for finished cloth. But the market for yarn was indeed large; and this was the one modern manufacture in which China rapidly developed substantial export capacity, despite the fact that the learning process in cotton spinning was denied even momentary protection by the unequal treaties.

With these additions, the Elvin–Perkins model becomes identical with my explanation of stagnation in a densely-populated poor economy. But that is not the end of the story. One can see why market forces could not sustain a spontaneous development process, but the puzzle of the state's inertia—its failure or refusal to perform a developmental role—remains unresolved.

Military Pressure and the Traditional Chinese State

The clue to this puzzle lies in the character of the Chinese state—which in turn is rooted in the facts of Chinese geography. The immensely long land frontier of China proper, though protected to the south-west and west by impassable mountains and deserts, lies open to the north. There it separates the agricultural civilization of the Hwang Ho basin from the pastoral nomads of the Inner Asian Steppe, whose mobile way of life predisposes them to migration and invasion especially when their grasslands dry up in the desiccation phase of our planetary weather cycle. Further, no natural barriers intervene between the northern border and the heartland of agri-cultural China. The north China plain and the fertile well-watered lower and middle basin of the Yangtze are topographically continuous and indivisible. No stable defence lines can be maintained anywhere on their level immensity. Yet the ebb and flow of battle across these vast spaces would so devastate the population and the economy that avoiding—or at least minimizing—this possibility becomes imperative for the survival of Chinese society. A unitary authority over this entire region, strong enough to suppress the rebel and repulse the invader, is thus a matter of geographic necessity. Once such an authority establishes itself in the vast rich Chinese heartland, it can marshal enough resources to control the periphery of China proper—the rugged valleys of the south-east and the fertile mountain-girt basin of Szechwan. Hence the immemorial unity of the Chinese Empire. Since the days of Ch'in Shi Hwang-Ti, over the aeons spanned by the Han, the Sui, the Tang, the Sung, the Yuan, the Ming, and the Ch'ing, with but a few brief spells of chaos and divisiveness, China proper has maintained her territorial integrity. History knows no comparable record of imperial unity over so vast a span of time and space.

The prime function that geography imposed on the Chinese state then was that of military security. And the structure of the state reflected its function. Effective mobilization required a unitary imperial order which brooked no competing centres of influence. Power was oriented northwards around Peking to facilitate the protection of the open north-west frontier. The sea and the south-east coast were neglected. Indeed, since Chinese political institutions crystallized long before the age of long distance ocean transport and the resulting threat from the sea, they positively discouraged maritime activity so as to forestall the emergence of a rival focus of power based on foreign trade. Up to the fifteenth century, a certain interest in ship-building and the navy was essential for the defence of the north: the northern capital and garrison had to be provisioned by sea from the surplus provinces of the south. This interest culminated in the great Ming voyages of 1405–33 under eunuch–admiral Ching Ho. But the completion of the Grand Canal extinguished all interest in the ocean and Ming China withdrew landwards behind a barrier of official bans on maritime activity and sometimes indeed on coastal settlement.

The monistic political system and the solidarity of the ruling class—the scholars and the gentry—were but part of the military design of the Chinese state. The other part was the ideology and the family system which supported it. The Confucian ethic offered a philosophical justification for the established order: it inculcated a doctrine of obedience to the powers that be, ranging from the paternal to the imperial. The authoritarian Chinese patriarchal family in turn tended to mould its members into the conservative and obedient citizenry on which a paternalistic empire thrives. Yet Confusianism never completely extinguished rival schools of thought; nor did the patriarchal family ever totally erode the dissident outlook. In the ultimate analysis, it was the logic of strategic compulsions, the perception of this logic by the ruling class, and its embodiment in political institutions that held the empire together.

The interest of the military state in technological and economic development ceased naturally at the point where a margin of military superiority over the invader from the north-west was assured. The intensity of the northern military challenge thus largely determined China's techno-economic response. It can be contended, for instance, that the innovative brilliance of the Sung era—which saw the development, among other things of firearms, the mariner's compass, and printing—can be explained by the relentless pressure of the Tartar and Mongol hordes.

But the desire to maintain an edge over the invader did not guarantee the ability to do so. In the last phase of a dynastic cycle—as described by Wittfogel (67)—population pressure would erode the tax base and intensify peasant rebelliousness; the military advantage of the regime over the invader would then melt away, and alien conquest often follow. This in fact is the point at which demographic and military pressure have traditionally interacted in shaping the destiny of China.

The endlessly shifting but essentially stable equilibrium between military threat and defence capability was rudely shattered in the nineteenth century by the growth of the European empires of the sea. What had been a protective moat to the East became suddenly a highway for invasion; and from this traditionally neglected direction an overwhelmingly superior military technology was brought to bear on the Heavenly Kingdom.

A shock of this magnitude was beyond the absorptive capacity of a regime attuned to the order of challenge of the nomadic invader. The political system was too rigid, too monolithic, too heavily burdened by the values of the past and the vested interests of the ruling class to adjust successfully to the western threat. Certainly, there was a response—characteristically on the purely military plane. This was the 'Self-Strengthening' movement—the attempt sponsored by Tseng Kuo-Fan, Li Hung-Chang, and others to improve military technology and ancillary industries without major changes in economic structure of political organization. It was, of course, pitifully inadequate for the circumstances of the nineteenth century. Government revenue was limited by the impossibility of taxing the rich and politically powerful scholar gentry class; the drain of this revenue into the hands of the microscopic mandarinate through organized corruption continued unabated; much of the residue was spent in merely feeding the army—so that government demand was never large enough to generate economies of scale in the ancillary industries. Much military equipment was, therefore, directly imported. Even where equipment was eventually produced at home (in arsenals and shipyards for example), the machinery for producing it continued to come from cheap mass producers abroad. The linkage effect of government demand thus overflowed abroad. Indeed, under the Manchu principle of 'government supervision and merchant operation', the private entrepreneur never had much incentive to invest anyway, since his profit was always at the mercy of the arbitrary exactions of the bureaucracy.

Without economic growth or organizational change, military self-strengthening never acquired its essential logistic basis. China's military weakness, therefore, persisted—as was dramatically demonstrated by the Sino-Japanese War of 1895 and the continued encroachment of the West culminating in the Boxer War (1900). Indeed, the imperial order was truly immutable. So completely did it resist all change from within that—even in its very last phase—it defied the reformist intensions of the Emperor himself. During the famous Hundred Days of 1898, the Emperor Kuang-Hsu—inspired by the Confucian reformer Kang Yu-Wei—sought to change the entire structure of Chinese society and the Chinese state by a series of imperial decrees. So powerful were the military and bureaucratic interests that had to be alienated in the process that, on the hundredth day, the Emperor was effectively deposed and imprisoned; the Manchu regime resumed its inexorable course towards nemesis under the regency of that arch-reactionary, the Dowager Empress.

The very factors that made the Empire so unchangeable also endowed it with an element of indestructibility. The solidarity of the élite—its united commitment to and stake in the old order—had enabled the Empire earlier to survive the great Malthusian crisis of the mid-nineteenth century. The long upswing of population had been accelerated in the nineteenth century by the mushrooming export demand for tea and silk from the Yangtze valley. By the 1850s rural China was in complete disarray. Over-population had sparked off a series of peasant revolts all over the country, the mightiest of which, the Taiping rebellion, engulfed the rich middle and lower Yangtze basin, established a new kingdom with its capital at Nanking, and cut off the Empire from its grain-revenues along the Grand Canal. Simultaneously, the Nien rebels established themselves in the country between the Yangtze and the Hwang Ho and Muslim rebellions flared up in Yunnan and the north-west. The recovery of the Empire from impending catastrophe was due in large measure to the loyalty of the scholar-gentry, to men like Tseng Kuo-Fan, Li Hung-Chang and Tso Tsung-Tang who organized local militias which slowly but inexorably exterminated the rebels. In this, they were helped by the weapons and tactics acquired from the West (so that self-strengthening stabilized the old order instead of changing it). They were also aided by the precarious balance of power between the western imperialists, which deterred any of them from exploiting China's disunity to establish a full-scale colonial regime. Meanwhile, this interregnum of bloody disorder drastically reduced population pressure; it thereby gave the Empire a reprieve of another half century from one of the twin forces for change in traditional China.

The Disintegration of Traditional China and the Rise of Communism

But military pressure on China continued unabated. And, by the beginning of the twentieth century, the population was proliferating again. What was more, the Chinese élite was no longer quite so monolithic. The expansion of maritime trade and contact with the West had nurtured new interest groups and centres of power. The treaty ports of Shanghai and Canton where merchants and manufactures, western education, and commercial law flourished under the shelter of extraterritoriality, the province of Kwangtung with its traditional maritime interests, the overseas Chinese communities, growing rapidly in numbers and affluence with Chinese overseas trade, all became important foci of power with little stake in the Manchu regime. It was from these centres that the Republican revolution drew its leadership and its main strength. Kang Yu-Wei, the Confucian reformer, Liang Chi-Chao, the more radical nationalist, and Sun Yat-Sen, the revolutionary, came alike from Kwangtung. They derived their support from Kwangtung and Hong Kong, the Communist organized Shanghai proletariat, and Chinese students and settlers in south-east Asia, Hawaii, the US, West Indies, and Europe. Sun's Government was restricted to Kwangtung till the Northern campaigns of Chiang Kai-shek in 1926–7; and the Kuomintang cabinets were highly cosmopolitan and westernized, with members like the celebrated Trinidad-born Eugene Chen, who knew not a word of Chinese.

   ˙ Yet, while commerce and western influence nurtured a rival élite, it remained essentially peripheral to Chinese society. It could direct the overthrow of the decadent Manchu empire, but not inherit its legacy. It had no link with rural China. It could not prevent the countryside from dissolving into warlord anarchy or mobilize effective resistance against the Japanese invader.

   In a sense, the interregnum between the two revolutions (1911–49) was of a piece with the whole pattern of Chinese history since the Taiping Rebellion. The basic political device that had held the vast empire together, despite the backwardness of its communications, was the division between the military and the revenue functions of the government. The warrior and the bureaucrat had separate but interdependent roles—so that neither could individually mount an effective challenge to central authority. The mid-nineteenth-century rebellions undermined this vital separation of powers. They necessitated the regionalization of the army—the formation of local militias under bureaucratic control— and so prepared the way for the rise of the warlords. The political structure of the Empire henceforth represented the feudal, rather than the bureaucratic, solution to the security problems of an agrarian society. It could not resist great centrifugal forces; and the disintegration of the Empire into a host of warring regional powers (which is what even the KMT and the Communists were before 1949) became inevitable. The fall of the Empire was thus a slow, two-stage process: first, the erosion of its bulwarks against feudal decentralization; second, the inevitable collapse of such a feudalistic authority structure into regional fragments which were not reunited till 1949.

   It was left to men of peasant origin from the impenetrable agricultural interior—Mao Tse-Tung and Liu Shao-Chi from Hunan and Chu Teh from Szechwan—to organize and direct the other great

revolutionary force of twentieth-century China—peasant discontent. The opening up of Manchuria at the beginning of this
century provided an outlet for the population pressure which so
afflicted the peasant economy. But, despite the astronomical increase in the population of Manchuria in the next four decades, the
resulting relief was but partial and temporary. It was swamped by
the effect on the death rate of the improvement in food-distribution
following the advent of the railroad. And Manchuria was pretty
much filled up by 1940. The all-pervasive impact of population
pressure on the rural economy was something that the urban,
commercial, and military interests represented by the Kuomintang
were not equipped to handle. Thus it was peasant revolution that
eventually conquered China. But it was a revolution dedicated not
only to the solution of the agrarian problem but also, unlike the
Taiping, to the classic objectives of the Chinese state—unity and
military security. And, since in the international environment of the
twentieth century, each of these aims requires an industrial-scientific revolution, this became a prime commitment of the new Chinese
state.

To recapitulate, the inertia of the Chinese state before the
Communist Revolution in the field of development was the result of
its structure. This structure in turn was determined by its traditional
function. The imperial state was a specialized adaptation to the
problem of security of a great continental region before the age of
ocean navigation. It was not designed to carry economic development any further than needed to repel Central Asian invaders and
maintain internal unity. Its monolithic character—logical enough
for its defensive function—made it incapable of rapid change from
within. When the population swelled beyond its absorptive capacity, the imperial order did not change; it dissolved instead into
chaos in which an invader or a new Chinese dynasty succeeded and
instituted the changes needed to accommodate a larger population.
The advent of western sea power made the imperial order militarily
obsolete. This distance of China from the centres of the western
military-industrial revolution meant that her exposure to the West
came about suddenly when western power was already full-blown.
There was no slow escalation of challenge which would leave the
Chinese state with time for a gradual adjustment. Sudden dramatic
change was called for and this the monolithic Empire could not
generate from within. Nor could the imperial order be destroyed in

the traditional manner of the dynastic cycle by the combination of military and population pressures. The rivalries of the western powers protected China from western conquest. And the acquisition of western weapons enabled the Empire to control internal rebellion as long as the élite remained monolithic. Thus the Empire survived as a living fossil until commerce and contact with the West nurtured a rival élite capable of overthrowing the Manchus, but not of the radical policies needed to satisfy the peasantry or unite and defend the country. Indeed, the development of a populous traditional economy like China's in the world of the twentieth century required a restoration—in fact a massive reinforement—of central power. This was all the more necessary because military pressure was so important a motive force behind Chinese development. But in its brief spells of even symbolic unity the Republic was too pluralistic to centralize power successfully; and, of course, in an overwhelmingly agrarian economy, it was too urban in its interests ever to wield the far-flung support that central power demands. Equally inappropriate was the urban proletarianism which Borodin and his associates sought to transplant in the Chinese soil. Indeed, when Maoism inherited the Chinese revolution, it did so because it alone represented an adequate response to the twin challenge of population explosion and military pressure on China's peasant economy.

II The Contours of Communist Development

Military and population pressures were the twin forces that propelled Imperial China to her long-delayed nemesis and the Communist Revolution to its eventual victory. These factors have continued to shape the destiny of China even after 1949. They have set the pattern of her economic development, and determined the direction and the oscillations of Communist policy.

Demographic Effects

The demographic compulsion on policy has two aspects. It enforces a concern with equity; and it accentuates the problem of maintaining minimal supplies of basic necessities—particularly of food. Population pressure on land and the resulting concentration of land ownership and agrarian income accounted in large measure for rural discontent in pre-Revolutionary China and for the peasant origins of the Communist Revolution. This in turn committed the Revolution to equalitarianism in theory and practice. The large-scale redistribution of land soon after the Communist take-over and the continuous preoccupation with equality in visible consumption standards are corollaries of this.

The problem of maintaining food supplies is much more intractable. Redistribution of course substantially improved mass nutrition; but the once for all possibilities of institutional change have been spent, and maintenance—not to speak of improvement—of food consumption in the face of continued population growth now calls for progressive increase in agricultural output. The problem here is that population pressure is the hardy perennial of the Chinese economy. Over centuries of such pressure, all opportunities for extension of cultivated acreage and increase of productivity per acre within the traditional technology have been explored and exhausted. The borders of China, too, have already been pushed beyond the limits within which the climate could support agriculture. Thus further output expansion requires a scientific revolution in agriculture—the large-scale application of chemical fertilizers, power-driven irrigation pumps, and other inputs of industrial origin. This implies industrialization. The role of industrialization is not just related to the production of agricultural inputs. It could also replace essential industrial imports, releasing foreign exchange for import of food, fertilizers, and the like. Alternatively, it would generate manufactured exports—of textiles and high-value processed foods—in exchange for cheap foreign grain.

China's natural resource endowment reinforces the case for industrialization as a response to population pressure. Land that can be cultivated is a scarce resource in China, but her mineral wealth is fabulous and largely unexploited. Her reserves of coal, iron, and petroleum are exceptional; she is among the world's largest producers of tin, tungsten, antimony, bismuth, mercury, molybdenum, salt, magnesite, asbestos, graphite, etc.; among major minerals, she is notably deficient only in nickel and chromium. Thus, mining and heavy industry based on it constitute an adaptation to China's comparative advantage; they involve a substitution of mineral-intensive activities for land-using ones. Indeed, China has not only developed her metal-processing industries at a spectacular rate; she is also a major exporter of metals.

The Consequences of Military Pressure

If population pressure dictates industrialization, military pressures reinforce this dictate. In the early years of the regime the military threat was perceived as coming from the United States as the heir to the maritime colonialist role of the western powers over the last century. But, since 1960, the ancient fears of the Chinese about their northern frontiers have revived. The increasing dependence of China on industry has itself intensified these fears, since the heavy industrial base of the economy is located in the northern border areas of Manchuria and Sinkiang.

The military orientation of the Chinese economy is reflected in the stress on heavy and basic industries. Coal, steel, petroleum, electric power, metal processing, and chemicals are the fastest growing sectors of Chinese industry; and, while there is little interest in exploiting this growing productive capacity to *increase* consumer welfare, there is overwhelming concern with mobilizing it for the purpose of military security. The massive investment in the acquisition of a credible nuclear deterrent and the vast industrial infra-structure this requires is the most important example of this.

This military orientation lends an underlying unity to Chinese policy. Its vacillations, on the other hand, are related to a division of opinion about the appropriate response to military pressure. The Maoist line is that China cannot hope in the near future to achieve technological parity in weaponry with her foes, and must therefore evolve a defensive strategy that capitalizes on manpower rather than weapons. The ideal strategy for her is rural guerrilla warfare. This requires the ability of each regional guerrilla stronghold to survive on its own, without depending on attenuated communication lines which an enemy can blockade, and a sense of solidarity between the army, the peasantry, and the political leadership. Hence, the advocacy of a cellular pattern of economic development (preserving the essential configuration of pre-industrial China) with regional self-sufficiency based on widely-dispersed small-scale industrialization. Also, the attempt to foster a sense of identification between the army, the party, and the peasantry by minimizing income differentials, insisting on work in the countryside as a part of the educational process, the politicization of the armed forces, the discouragement of professionalism and technical expertise in work and in educational curricula. The emphasis is on general-purpose versatility rather than hierarchal work relations, on ideological exhortation rather than material incentives, on a populist rather than a professional army.

Counterposed against this is the alternative strategic model which assumes that the guerrilla strategy—while inevitable before the Revolution—is now much too expensive a technique of defence. It involves the surrender of the periphery of China (including Manchuria and Sinkiang) and of her urban-industrial regions. The alternative would be accelerated heavy industrialization with a military bias and the fullest development of the nuclear deterrent to reduce the technological gap between the Chinese and the Soviet armies as rapidly as possible. This in turn would require concentration and large scale of industry, a well-developed transport network, high levels of skill and military professionalism (fostered by technical education and material incentives), and well-defined chains of command. It would avoid the costs of the Maoist model in terms of diseconomies of small scale, of regional autarky, of industrial indiscipline, and of lack of specialized skills. While the issue is not yet clear, perhaps the economic advantages of this alternative have led to the eclipse of the Maoist model.

The costs of industrialization and defence impose on China a regime of spartan austerity—though an essential minimum is guaranteed to all. In turn, military necessity and economic austerity both require an authoritarian political system. All these are aspects of China which are well known and widely commented upon. The essential difference here with an economy like the Indian—where the demonstration effect is a prime mover of growth—will be spelled out later. The military—as distinct from economic—function of Chinese authoritarianism has already been discussed. These are, therefore, issues which need not be elaborated here.

Finally the closure of the economy minimizes popular discontent with such a spartan regime by sealing off the people from the demonstration effect of western goods. However, with population pressure compelling a dependence on foreign food and the increasing exploitation of China's mineral wealth for exports, the existing rifts in the Bamboo Curtain are likely to widen.

10

DEVELOPMENT CONTRASTS: RUSSIAN, JAPANESE, AND INDIAN DEVELOPMENT MEASURED AGAINST THE CHINESE MODEL

I Russia

Motive Forces of Russian and Chinese Development

THE Russian mode of economic development bears the closest resemblances to the Chinese. The compulsions behind growth in Russia were of the same military and demographic varieties as in China. There was the military threat that modern industrial states posed to a backward Russia—so vividly highlighted by the Russian débâcles in Crimea (1834), in Manchuria (1903), and in the First World War. There was the population explosion of the nineteenth century. The Revisions, as they were called, indicate a growth in numbers from about 14 million in the 1720s to 74 million by 1858, making Russia the third most populous country in the world (Blum (4)).

Of course, the density of the population relative to total surface area was, and still is, low. But so acute were the geographical constraints on agriculture that this figure was of little significance. The brevity of the growing season made most of northern Russia uncultivable. To the south and east, in the continental interior of Russia, aridity had the same effect. The land sloped northwards, so that most rivers flowed down to the largely ice-bound Arctic: their lower courses remained frozen while their headwaters thawed, resulting in floods and marshy conditions over vast areas through much of the spring and summer growing seasons. Such a climate in turn depleted the soil, producing acid soils in the marshy north and a tendency to alkalinity in the arid south-east. These conditions severely restricted the arable area—both directly and through the problems they posed for transport and settlement in a non-industrial economy. Hence the obsession of nineteenth–and early twentieth-century Russia with 'the agrarian problem'—with low incomes and underemployment among the peasantry.

On the other hand, export expansion was no more a dynamic

factor in Russia than in China. The grain surpluses extracted from the Czarist peasantry in the late nineteenth century were competed out of the world market by the deluge of cheap wheat from the emptier lands of the American mid-West.

Nor was the demonstration effect in consumption a significant moving force in either Russia or China. The masses were but little exposed to foreign goods; and the ruling élite—though more open to the influence of such goods—lived in a world apart without any intervening classes through which their example could filter down to the vast majority of the population. In the twentieth century, of course, the mass media might possibly have broken the isolation of the Russian and Chinese peoples, but the Communist regimes artificially perpetuated this isolation by drawing an Iron Curtain around themselves—so that, except in Russia after Stalin, the demonstration factor has been negligible.

Similarities in Growth Patterns

The consequent similarities in development patterns between the two countries are obvious. The stress on heavy industrialization with a military bias, the autarchic economic pattern, the all-embracing role of the state in economic activity, the frenzied pace of the growth effort, the enforced austerity in consumption, the intense concentration of economic and political power—are all common characteristics of Czarist and Soviet development no less than of China since 1949. Of further interest is the convergence of both countries to Communism. The Czarist regime—unlike the non-Communist governments of China—initiated modern economic development but precipitated in the process its own dissolution. The necessities of development implied the severest pressure on mass consumption. Such sacrifice may be borne for the sake of the future security or affluence of the nation—but only if the people at large feel at one with the state. A minimal degree of popular acquiescence in crushing tax-burdens requires some sense of identification between the citizen and his government. Czarist Russia sought to promote this through the patriarchal Orthodox model of the Czar as 'the little father' of his people. The myth unfortunately became increasingly divorced from reality. The Czar and the nobility lived in a world apart, with consumption levels astronomically different from those of their other subjects. They embroiled the country in costly and lethal wars of no apparent relevance to the average Russian—such as the wars of 1903–5 and 1914–17. And when the unarmed citizenry petitioned him for the redress of grievances, they were mowed down by gunfire as at the winter palace in Petrograd 1905. So profound an alienation in reality could hardly support the myth of unity of monarch and people in one happy family. And with ideology failing in its function of reconciling the people to their government, the sanction of force became all important as the basis of authority. In 1917, the disintegration of the morale of the army coincided with economic pressures on the populace and the regime crumbled before a tide of popular discontent that it lacked the means to control.

In contrast to Czarism, Communist theory and practice provided an infinitely more convincing rationale for the austerities of the development process. Equalitarianism—the minimizing of visible inequalities in consumption, the broadening of the avenues for upward mobility—tended to foster a certain sense of identification between the people and the élite. The distribution of power remained utterly skewed of course—that indeed was another imperative of development; but it was more open than before, and the myth of 'the dictatorship of the proletariat' may even have beguiled the gullible into overlooking the true measure of concentration of personal power at the top of the political pyramid. The functions of Communist ideology in China were roughly similar.

Developmental Contrasts

Despite these broad similarities, the tempo and pattern of growth in China and Russia show some interesting differences. Thus, the Czarist regime initiated the typical development process I have described, but pre-Communist China did not. The military pressures on Czardom came from a familiar quarter; the response in terms of heavy industrialization under Vyshnegradskii and Witte was simply a reversion to the older Petrine model. In China, the impact of the West was more traumatic. In an empire attuned for millennia to the defence of the northern land border, the challenge of the intruder from the sea had an altogether different and unfamiliar order of magnitude. An overwhelmingly superior force had suddenly appeared on China's doorstep—and no constructive response was therefore possible. In all this, the Russian situation was of course quite different.

Thanks to the surges of Czarist industrialization, the Soviets inherited a far more substantial heavy industrial base and a larger proletariat than did the CCP. Further, given the large-scale, concentrated pattern of industry, the bulk of the 6 million railway, mining, and factory workers (in 1915) were clustered around large urban-industrial complexes. Here was a fertile soil for proletarian revolutionary movements. Nothing comparable existed in China outside Shanghai. The Chinese economy in 1949 was still almost totally agrarian, and the revolution depended entirely on a peasant army. This difference in the structure of the two economies and consequently in the balance of power within the revolutionary movement was reflected in different views of the relationship between agriculture and industry. The traditional Russian preoccupation with the peasant problem from Tolstoy to Chayanov had its Soviet counterpart in Bukharin's advocacy of development through increased demand. But it was Preobrazhensky, the protagonist of super-industrialization, who triumphed. Throughout the Stalin era, agriculture was regarded simply as the source of surpluses ruthlessly extracted to feed the growing proletariat. Stalinist agricultural policy focused single-mindedly on maximizing procurement rather than output. Collectivization, compulsory deliveries, and the like were all instruments to this end. They took their terrible toll of the peasant and left as Stalin's legacy a stagnant and inefficient agriculture and a wide income differential between farm and factory. In China, on the other hand, the peasant roots of power—particularly military power—were always strong enough to rule out a ruthless exploitation of agriculture. The economic and military arguments for rapid industrialization at the expense of agriculture existed—but they were countered by the Maoist ideological and guerrilla strategic considerations already mentioned. The farmer in the Soviet Union has been relegated to a marginal role; but in China he continues to occupy the centre of the stage—today, as he has done throughout the measureless past.

II Japan

Population and Military Pressures in China and Japan

One of the most striking problems in Asian history is the contrast in the dynamics of development between China and Japan. The contrast is all the more remarkable because it was superimposed on a similarity of motive forces for growth. In Japan—as in China—population pressure was a vital stimulus. There is, of course, some controversy over whether Japan's population had stabilized in the mid-Tokugawa era at 25–30 millions (Taeuber (59), Hanley and Yamamura (23)). But there is little doubt that it was rising from the 1840s. By the eve of the Restoration, it had probably passed 35 million; in a small, mountainous,infertile country, the resulting pressure on the land was unbearable.

Simultaneously, moreover, Japan—like China—was exposed to the full blast of western expansionism. Beginning with Perry's penetration of her isolation, western pressure on Japan mounted in a rapid crescendo. The Treaty of Kanagawa with the United States was followed by those of Nagasaki with the British and of Shimoda with the Russians; the French and the Dutch did not lag far behind. All this culminated in the Tariff Convention of 1866 which limited Japan's external tariff to 5 per cent. The treaties were as unequal as those imposed on China in forcing extra-territoriality and denying tariff autonomy; and they remained in force right through the crucial period of Meiji industrialization in the nineteenth century. They constitute, therefore, a decisive refutation of the popular thesis that the stagnation of Manchu China resulted from the dislocation caused by western commercial imperialism through the unequal treaties—the decay of Chinese handicrafts due to the competition of imported manufacures and the like.

The Differential Effects of Geography

Given the similarity in the compulsions for growth, what accounts for the very different patterns and tempi of response in these two closely related societies? We suggest that in the ultimate analysis these differences are rooted in geography. Japan's insular character affected the speed of her modernization in two vital ways. First, the proximity of all parts of the country to the ocean, the sheltered harbours, the landlocked lines of internal navigation provided by the Inland Sea, all combined to ensure a rapid diffusion of external maritime influences. In an age when water transport technology was more advanced than land transport, military pressures and commercial opportunities originating from the outside world could be felt in every corner of Japan and imported manufactures penetrated the furthest recesses of the domestic economy. In contrast, much of continental China long retained its virgin inaccessibility to foreign influence; and it was this that constituted the unyielding core of the imperial system. The Yangtze waterway was the main axis of foreign penetration into the interior of China. Alongside it, tea and silk production for export mushroomed from the 1840s; and within a decade of the Opium War, the lower Yangtze provinces generated—in the Taiping rebellion—the most dramatic challenge to its survival that the Empire was to face. Indeed, the history of the nineteenth century would have been quite different if the Yangtze basin had been all there was of China.

But it was not only by regulating the speed and scale of western penetration that geography affected the relative durability of the two empires. It also influenced their political structure. In continental China, with its immense land frontier, external security as well as internal unity demanded a single focus of power. Japan, with its island immunity to invasion, needed centralization less; she could afford a polycentric state. The Ch'ing state was a monolithic empire with a single well-defined chain of command; but the Tokugawa was a pluralistic feudal system with a multiplicity of carefully balanced centres of power. The lack of competing foci of influence made the Chinese system resistant to changes that came easily in Japan. The Japanese warrior class indeed was permanently divided. It contained elements which were inherently alienated from the Tokugawa *bakufu* and constituted natural sources of discord in the feudal order. These were the four western *han:*

1. Satsuma in south-west Kyushu, almost encircled by the sea and enriched by a contraband trade with China via an administrative post it maintained in the Ryukyu Islands;
2. Hizen, the hinterland of Nagasaki—exposed through this window on the world to the demonstration effect and the commercial influence of the West;
3. Choshu in western Honshu, guarding the Straits of Shimonoseki, the western outlet of the Inland Sea and the potential link between the ocean trade routes and the inland commerce of Japan;
4. Tosa in southern Shikoku, the southern water-front of Japan on the Pacific.

All four outer *han* faced naturally seawards; they had a keener awareness of the outside world than the rest of Japan even during the Tokugawa isolation; they stood to gain substantially from an expansion of internal and foreign trade; and they were protected by distance from the centre of *shogunal* power. Their distinctive position had been recognized and embodied in the settlement of Tokugawa Iyeasu after the battle of Sekigahara. The settlement— while conceding them a measure of autonomy and the right of access to the emperor—denied them any share in the central administration and enforced their subservience through a well-known system of complicated constraints. The western clans were misfits in the *shogunal* system, an alienated élite; and when opportunity arose, they became the spearhead of revolution.

The alienation of the outer *han* was shared in some degree by the lower *samurai* everywhere. A functionless and impoverished élite, they were banned in principle from land ownership or mercantile activity by the feudal restrictions on occupational mobility; and, even when some of them succeeded in penetrating these occupations, they found the road to riches beset by feudal constraints (e.g. on the sale of land) and the monopoly privileges of the rich Osaka merchants—to whom the *shogun* and the *daimyo* were deeply indebted.

Large segments of the political and military élite were thus in a state of perennial discontent. When the mid nineteenth-century crisis erupted, their rebelliousness struck a responsive chord in other broad strata of the population. Population pressure in the countryside had by then led both to a decline in average land holdings and standards of living and to a progressive differentiation and concentration of rural wealth. The poor had survived by supplementing their income by handicrafts—until the flood of western manufactures in the wake of the unequal treaties disrupted the village economy. The rural rich—the larger peasants and usurers and the traders in rural handicrafts—remained disaffected because of their lack of social status and political power.

But if the Meiji revolutionaries rode the whirlwind of rural discontent, the speed of their success was due largely to the divisions within the established élite—and indeed to the leadership of segments of the élite in the revolutionary struggle. In China, by contrast, the established leadership of the Empire was homogeneous, and therefore indissolubly wedded to the established order.

An implication of this is that the conflict of 1868 followed the vertical cleavage lines in Japanese society. It did not, therefore,

generate an egalitarian ideology; nor did it lead to a major redistribution of established wealth, though the commercialization of
feudal rights and relationships did, of course, have its distributional
consequences. The Chinese political system lacked such vertical
cleavages; it could split only along horizontal strata. Hence the need
for an egalitarian philosophy to rationalize revolution in China.
Hence, also, the large-scale redistribution of wealth that followed
it.

Japan's Export Success: Its Political–Economic Consequences and its Causes

If nineteenth-century Japan differed from China in the speed with
which it found a new political equilibrium, the stability of this equilibrium depended on the rapid success of the new regime in resolv-
ing the problems that destroyed the *shogunate*. Indeed, the first
decade of Meiji was more tempestuous than any of the Tokugawa
era with *samurai* discontent exploding in the Satsuma Rebellion and
the peasantry in continuous—if localized—revolt. Without a rapid
alleviation at least of agrarian discontent, Japan could not have
averted chaos and eventual class war *à la* China. But in fact the
burden on the peasantry progressively lightened. The land tax—
though initially as onerous as the Tokugawa levies and more inflex-
ible in times of distress—was fixed in money terms and left un-
touched the increment in peasant productivity. Further, its real
value declined as the price of rice rose: and, even in the depths of
the depression of 1884–5, rice prices remained well above their
initial 1873 levels (Smith (58)). Meanwhile, the peasant could sup-
plement his income through raw silk production for export and
expanding industrial employment opportunities for his family
members. Thus, from the second half of the 1880s, peasant discontent and rebelliousness subsided and the Meiji political order
was stabilized.

   There were two elements in this relatively rapid transition: the
disengagement of government from direct industrial production
and investment in the 1880s—which reduced the fiscal burden; and
the emergence of private enterprise which exploited the infra-
structure of communications and training facilities established by
government, the sale of government industries at nominal prices,
and, above all, the expanding export market to sustain and even
accelerate economic growth. Thus, from the second decade of

Meiji, the Japanese development pattern begins to diverge from the agonizing process of government-dominated industrialization. The close partnership of industry and government continued, particularly in the domain of heavy industry, but there was now little direct government involvement in production and spontaneous market forces powered the spectacular expansion of light industry into the export area.

Even Japan's success, however, was related to the catalytic role of government. Japan's export potential derived from certain limited natural advantages (in raw silk) and an abundant labour supply. The Meiji government sought to capitalize on both. Its support for quality-control and standardization in raw silk production and the mechanization of silk-reeling enabled Japan to oust her main rival, China, from the world market. Its support for the labour-intensive cotton textile industry—through training facilities, model plants, and the like—facilitated its growth from an import-substituting industry to a substantial exporter. Proximity to the large continental market was, of course, a major stimulus to the cotton textile industry—at least in its competition with the western and Indian industries. Yet, here again, the political factor—the existence in Japan, but not in China, of a regime wedded to economic development— was decisive, since factor proportions in China were no less favourable for cotton textile production. Fortuitous accidents—silk-worm disease in Europe in the 1880s and the plague of 1896 in Bombay which resulted in the exclusion of Indian cotton textiles from the Chinese market—also played a part.

Export, Empire, and Natural Resources in Japan and China

Japan's export expansion, however, was less important as a continuing injection of new demand into the economy than as an adaptation to her limited natural resource base. She was critically dependent on primary imports to sustain the momentum of her growth. This imposed both a compulsion to export, and an incentive to empire-building. An empire represented both a cheap source of raw materials and a captive market in which to earn the wherewithal for exports. Militant imperialism and export expansion were alternatives for Japan. Periods of rapid and unrestricted growth in world trade were accompanied by pacific and relatively democratic politics within Japan, while a restrictive and recessionary trade climate made for fascist government and imperialist expansion.

China's primary resource endowment is far richer, particularly in minerals, and Chinese economic development has less need accordingly of exports or of empire. This indeed is the last crucial difference in the development patterns of the two economies.

III India

Difference in the Degree of Western Penetration

The process of Indian economic development differs from the Chinese experience mainly on account of the differences in the colonial history of the two countries. The Mughal Empire—like the Manchu, a great land empire with its essentially subcontinental orientation—had run through its dynastic cycle a century earlier. It had crumbled under the pressure of new centres of power nurtured by the growing maritime trade of the remote south-west coast of India in the sanctuary beyond the western ghats. By the mid-eighteenth century, Mughal rule had dissolved in anarchy and the East India Company was poised to pre-empt the empire. At the time, the Ch'ing emperor Chien-Lung was commending King George III of the barbarians for his spirit of respectful submissiveness. It was not until 1842 that the western military presence made itself felt in China. The British conquest of India was by then complete. But the incentives for British empire-building in China were weak; British economic development had passed the phases of mercantilism and textile-based industrialization. China, therefore, was no longer very important to Britain as a source of exports or a market for textiles; and her poverty and geographical dispersion meant that she could not be a market for very much else. On the other hand, the costs of conquering and controlling another vast empire along attenuated communication lines across several thousand more miles of sea must have seemed forbidding for Britain. As for the other western nations, the balance of power precluded any unilateral colonial venture—so that the Manchu regime survived as a tottering relic right into the twentieth century. Thus, while India experienced direct colonial rule in fullest measure, the western impact on China remained localized and peripheral.

Resulting Contrasts in the Propellants of Growth

The consequences for development in the two economies were dramatic. While China remained vitally if ineffectually interested in defence and territorial unity, India abdicated these concerns to her colonial rulers. Even after Independence and Partition, India could seek the solution of her security problems in non-alignment and the bipolar global balance of power. Military pressure—the most powerful driving force behind Chinese industrialization—was a relatively insignificant factor in the Indian case.

On the other hand, India was penetrated by western trade, transport, and urbanization far more deeply than China. Plantation, mines, railways, commercial, administrative and educational structures on the western model were transplanted in the Indian milieu. They nurtured an urban middle-income group of white-collar workers, professionals and intellectuals as well as a significant class of indigenous capitalists. A continuous social hierarchy evolved in place of a society sharply polarized between a minute élite and a vast poor undifferentiated mass. The hierarchy determined social aspirations and acted as a channel through which the demonstration effect of new goods and ways of life filtered down to the lower strata of society. The demands of the highly articulate urban middle class and of aspirants to middle-class status for larger earning opportunities and superior consumption patterns were thus potent forces in India's modern history. So were the interests of the native capitalist class—which had grown up around the urban industrial sector. Indeed the Indian independence movement—and the Congress Party which was its main medium—originated in the demands of the urban middle class and the indigenous capitalists. It was only in the 1920s that a peasantry deeply affected by the beginnings of a population explosion was inducted into the movement by Gandhi. The resulting triple alliance was epitomized by the trinity that led the Congress in 1947—Ghandi with his insight into the peasant mind, Nehru the leader of the middle class, and Patel with his loyalties to the indigenous bourgeoisie. In China, the role of the urban middle class and the native capitalists was marginal to the Chinese heartland (though they did play an important part in the collapse of the Ch'ing) and the demonstration effect in consumption was negligible. The peasantry—or more specifically an army recruited from and dependent on the peasantry—set the tone and temper of the Communist Revolution.

Consequences for the Growth Patterns of the Two Economies

The peasant and guerrilla origins of the new Chinese Communist regime accounted for its strongly egalitarian ideology and policies, its overwhelming concern with the equitable redistribution of land, and the narrowing of income differentials. In India, on the other hand, land reform was confined to the dispossession of the absentee landlord, and equality was visualized not as a levelling of the income distribution but as a broadening of opportunities for upward mobility along a well-differentiated social structure. An expansion of educational opportunities and special privileges in legislative representation, education, and employment for backward castes and classes were aimed essentially at satisfying the aspirations of the poor to middle-class status.

The importance of the demonstration effect and the relative insignificance of military pressures in Indian economic development as compared to Chinese is reflected in the wider role and more diversified character of light consumer industry in India. The demonstration factor also accounts for the outward orientation of the Indian economy. Throughout the last thirty years, India has remained open, if not to consumer imports, certainly to foreign ideas and examples, to mass media and literature from abroad and direct intellectual exchanges. Conversely, the brain drain has assumed the proportions of an export industry, and the structure of Indian higher education itself has become export-oriented in this sense. In sharp contrast, China has been screened off from the outside world by the Bamboo Curtain. Her people have been insulated from the example of foreign goods and living standards—so that a demonstration effect, hitherto non-existent, does not emerge to intensify popular discontent with the austerity of the Communist regime. Nor is there a leakage of local skills abroad or a structure of education geared at least partially to export of skilled personnel.

All this has its implications for the choice of development strategies in the two economies. In India, the proliferation of the middle class through the expansion of the bureaucracy, the educational establishment, and the army and the consequent growth of a mass market for manufactures is one of the most distinctive features of development. So is the support of the investment incentives of the indigenous bourgeoisie through protection, subsidy, government contracts, and the like. In China, neither of these elements is a part of the design for development. The problem of investment incentives is resolved through direct social ownership of the means of production.

In India, the distribution of power is complex and multipolar as is characteristic of a commercialized society. It is incompatible with the centralization of economic power under full-scale socialism or of political power under a truly authoritarian dictatorship. Democracy—as the only form of compromise, however inefficient, between a diversity of evenly balanced groups and classes—continues to be the only viable political mode.

In China, of course, military pressures and a simpler class structure have led to a far more intense concentration of power. Society and the economy are organized along monolithic military lines despite the countercurrents generated by the Maoist guerrilla principles. Power here flows from the barrel of the gun and is consolidated by the concurrent centralization of economic and political authority in a socialist dictatorship.

These contrasts flow from differences in the motive forces of growth in the two economies. Other differences stem from the differential endowments of natural resources. The mineral base of China is far richer than that of India—both in metals and fuels. This has three implications. First, it means that China is better equipped for heavy industrialization than India. Secondly, it assures China of a larger export potential in minerals and mineral-based products and hints at a possibility that some semblance of export-led growth may eventually emerge in certain sectors of the chinese economy. Thirdly, it implies that the natural resource constraint may be less severe in the future development of China than of India. Agriculture will, of course, continue to be a problem in both economies. But, while China may be able to sustain her expansion by oil exports (say) to pay for food imports, India will have no comparable natural resource advantage in exports. The 'stop-go' mechanism of food and raw material scarcity cutting short every wave of expansion will continue its relentless operation in the Indian economy.

11

THE NATURE AND THE FUTURE OF
INTERNATIONAL ECONOMIC INEQUALITY

*International Economic Inequality and the Age of Economic
Development*

THE pattern of global economic growth shows two striking discontinuities, one in space, the other in time. The spatial discontinuity is the gulf between the rich nations and the poor. The temporal discontinuity is the great divide of the eighteenth century, which separates the era of modern economic growth from all earlier history. So astronomical in proportions are these gaps that one wonders whether they may not be examples of that elusive concept—the quantitative difference large enough to constitute a qualitative leap.

The astounding arithmetic of international economic disparity has been commented upon widely enough. In their consumption of material goods and services, the Atlantic community, Japan, Australia, and New Zealand are as far apart from the rest of the world's peoples as the inhabitants of another planet. It may not, of course, be impossible for the poorer nations to improve their living standards, but the costs in terms of present austerity and coercion of doing so are in most cases beyond imagination.

Quite as spectacular as the geographic division is the historical watershed of the eighteenth century. The unprecedented character of the rates of growth of various economies over the last two hundred years has been vividly stressed by Kuznets (34). He has shown that, if their contemporary growth rates are extrapolated backwards into the past, even the richest nations of today would appear to have been at minimal subsistence levels of *per capita* income (of $100 or less) two to three hundred years ago.

This explosive acceleration is not merely a matter of GNP growth, but also of an unprecedented population explosion. Despite this, the growth spurt of the last two centuries has systematically outstripped the explosive possibilities of population, so that growth has assumed an intensive rather than a merely extensive character. For the first time in history, there has been a long-sustained and large-scale rise in *per capita* income and standards of living on the one hand, and life expectancies on the other.

These two discontinuities—the spatial and the temporal—are, of course, intimately related, for the spectacular growth rates of the past two hundred years were not general global phenomena. They were highly localized: western Europe and North America led, followed by Japan—while other countries lagged well behind. The international inequalities of today are the legacy of these two hundred years of uneven development. Any interpretation of this therefore must focus on an explanation of two questions: the unevenness of modern economic growth and the specific locale where it first emerged. A third problem which one hopes to resolve relates to the unprecedented speed of the process.

The Two Causes of Poverty

To begin with the first of these questions: why was the present phase of world economic development so unbalanced regionally? Why did it not diffuse itself world-wide as the doctrine of comparative advantage would seem to dictate?

An answer to this riddle requires a distinction between two groups of poor countries—those that are sparsely populated in relation to their natural resource endowment and those that are densely populated. The delay in development of the thinly populated but resource-rich countries would be primarily a function of technology. Thus transport networks are not uniformly dense world-wide. The advent of modern economic growth followed upon a revolution in ocean transport, which was not matched by a transformation of communications over land until long afterwards. The initial pattern of economic development was inevitably littoral. Even when the land transport revolution came, it impinged first on countries with relatively inviting interiors. The forbidding heart of compact land masses like Africa, Australia, South America, and Central Asia with their deserts and equatorial forests remained essentially unexplored till recent times. The lag in the development of such hinterlands then is merely a reflection of the delayed development of land transport technology. These regions constitute the frontier of the world economy, towards which development will in the long run inevitably gravitate.

The overcrowded poor countries are an entirely different story. As suggested earlier, they do not have a place in the international trading system. Population pressure on their natural resources is too intense to permit them to develop—in competition with the empty countries—a sufficient volume and variety of primary exports to engulf the whole economy. Manufactures, on the other hand, are undermined by the smallness of the domestic market. The small home market makes it impossible for domestic manufacturers to realize economies of scale in processing without heavy dependence on exports with their high distribution costs, tariffs, and political uncertainties. They are, therefore, ousted by rivals based on the mass markets of richer countries. The populous poor nations, then, are unable to acquire a significant comparative advantage in either primary or industrial exports. They have, of course, a massive export potential in unskilled labour services.

Indeed, in a world without national boundaries, their primary function would have been as reservoirs from which unskilled labour flows out to locations better fitted for agricultural and industrial production—and keeps flowing until the pressure there has fallen to a level where comparative advantage in some broad range of activities can be sustained. The principle of national sovereignty rules all this out. The immigration restrictions of the richer countries exclude the poor populous nations from their natural role in the world economy as exporters of unskilled labour.

The continued poverty of the populous countries then reflects two facets of their legacy from the past—their high population densities and their poverty itself. The first of these factors makes them inefficient primary producers relative to the empty countries, the second makes them inefficient manufacturers compared to the rich countries. But the two factors are logically on different planes. Population density can indeed be regarded as an independent determinant of *per capita* income, but, if poverty is invoked as the basis of continued poverty, the problem of explanation is simply pushed back into the past. A general equilibrium model of the world economy might, of course, begin with international differences in capital endowment per head (as well as population densities)—but these are themselves the heritage of centuries of differential accumulation and one is left without a clue to this historical process. One understands why the empty countries may have prospered. But how, one wonders, did the rich densely-populated countries of today make their fortunes, even while other populous countries stagnated?

America and the Growth of the West

The answer, of course, is America. For populous western Europe, the discovery of the New World and the ocean trade routes of the fifteenth and sixteenth centuries opened up a vast virgin territory rich beyond imagination in natural resources which could serve both as an outlet for her surplus population and an opportunity for international specialization on a scale hitherto undreamt of. Post-Columbine economic history is therefore an entirely different proposition from pre-Columbine. It was of course centuries before western Europe could organize itself politically and technologically for the exploitation of the New World. But, right from the seventeenth century, the new sea routes are the overriding fact in western European history, the looming presence which overshadows all European events and processes. The growth of the mercantile classes, the emergence of the mercantilist state, the shift in the balance of power from the Mediterranean to the Atlantic, the wars for the mastery of the sea, the Commercial and ultimately the Industrial Revolutions—all reflect the importance of oceanic commerce and constitute, as it were, the preparation for the integration of the western European and the New World economies into the present system of international trade. Three hundred years of European history move inexorably towards this grand finale.

It was the completion of this commercial network and the establishment of undisputed political authority over it by a single state which generated—from the late eighteenth century—the unprecedented acceleration of growth in the Atlantic world. The conditions for the emergence of an entirely new pattern of international specialization and mass migration were guaranteed; now the mere unfolding of this pattern touched off explosive growth in the participating economies, growth which, for the first time in history, far surpassed even the meteoric rise of population. The virgin continent had exorcised the Malthusian devil.

The possibilities of this development pattern have not yet been fully exploited—as the difference in population pressures, export patterns, and standards of living between the two sides of the Atlantic indicates. And no doubt in future it will be extended to other less intensively utilized parts of the world. But what of the peoples that were left behind in this process? What of the sophisticated and populous civilizations of east and south Asia which—once they had surrendered an initial lead to western Europe—found themselves doomed to stagnation by the cumulative effects that continuously reinforced this disparity?

The most persistent of these cumulative processes operated through the market. It was set in train—as already suggested—by economies of scale in manufacturing. But more important—in the critical early phases of contact between the West and the East— were the self-reinforcing consequences of Europe's military superiority. It was the force of superior arms that established and maintained the political hegemony of the West in Asia and Africa with its corollaries of plunder and tribute, of unequal commercial treaties, and forcible suppression of Oriental industry. The military superiority of the West was in part a function of its economic superiority, at least from the eighteenth century. But it also contained an element that existed earlier in the seventeenth and late sixteenth centuries—an element that assured western arms of an advantage even in the heyday of Mughal, Manchu or Tokugawa glory. In fire power and naval warfare, the West had always ruled supreme, and both these technological advantages were developed through the intense naval competition among European states precipitated by the discovery of the New World and the new sea routes. Thus, European military superiority was itself related to Europe's deep involvement with the New World.

The crucial question then concerns the basis of Europe's advantage over Asia in relations with the New World. Proximity itself counted for much. Indeed, even within Europe, it produced a decisive shift in the focus of economic and political power from the Mediterranean to the Atlantic—from Renaissance Italy first to the intermediate kingdoms of Spain and Portugal with their footholds on both seas and ultimately to England and the Dutch Republic. But, apart from the facts of distance there was the maritime character of European geography. Europe is less a continent than a peninsula, composed indeed of lesser peninsulas. Its very high proportion of coastline to surface area contrasts sharply with the compact land mass of the densely-populated parts of Asia. For Europe, therefore, the sea was the natural highway of expansion while the great population centres of India and China remained preoccupied with their continental hinterlands. Muslim India was expanding irrigated agriculture while the West explored the sea. In a sense it was the very adaptability of India and China to the older continental way of life, their capacity to support vast populations without drastic technological transformation, that deterred them from the search for a radically new avenue to power and productivity. The biological analogue is obvious: one recalls the many species whose success in adapting to one set of circumstances itself delayed and impaired response when those circumstances changed. Thus, when the first western traders arrived in imperial India or China, they were treated with all the gracious condescension that barbarous tributaries may expect from the monarch of all heaven and earth. The Empires, firmly committed to their still flourishing ways of life, remained oblivious to the emerging danger from the sea. For them, the bell had tolled; but none, alas, heard or heeded.

The Meaning and Measurement of Economic Growth

What do we mean by economic growth? I have postponed this portentous semantic question till the last, partly because we all recognize certain historical processes as growth without having to venture into the labyrinth of definitions; but it is a question that must be faced because it spans an area in which language has been used persistently to cloud thinking rather than to clarify it. Specifically, we all tend to believe that with growth the welfare of the typical individual should increase. Indeed, we assert that increase in individual welfare is the criterion of growth. Yet there is no indication whatsoever that the processes which we describe as growth fulfil the criterion that we set up for it. Indeed, it may be argued that there is, even in principle, no way of ascertaining whether or not the criterion has been fulfilled in any given historical case. We are thus enmeshed in a linguistic web of contradictions of our own making; but we take no notice and cling lovingly to our twin dogmas about the process and the criterion of economic development.

Clearly, the picture that we have of economic growth at the back of our minds is very different from what we profess it to be. Our professed picture of it is a rationalization: it is coloured by what we feel is the compelling necessity for moral justification and is couched as such in terms of our prevailing utilitarian ethic. It is also a picture that bears no visible resemblance to the realities that we instinctively recognize as growth.

Let us explore the sources of this paradox in greater detail. The traditional interpretation of growth—as I have already said—is in terms of increase in individual welfare. This is reflected in the higher utility valuation of the changed basket of goods enjoyed by the typical individual.

The empirical measure based on this criterion of growth is the rise in *per capita* income. There are, of course, a number of familiar problems in the representation of individual welfare by *per capita* income. The imputation problem, the index number problem, the income distribution problem, etc., are well known. So is Boulding's (6) broader question as to whether welfare depends more on the current flow of output or on the enjoyment of the stock of durables (including natural and human resources, the environment, etc.) whose services do not necessarily correlate closely with their depreciation rate. Important though these problems are, I am not at present concerned with them. I assume them away in order to make the best possible case for the *per capita* income measure and to concentrate instead on the more basic question as to whether the historical process which we describe as growth can be legitimately understood in terms of increase in individual welfare.

A larger basket of goods, of course, leaves the individual happier given an invariant and unsaturated utility function. With a single or a Hicksian composite commodity, the assumptions of stability of tastes and non-satiety make this definitionally true. With many commodities not necessarily varying in the same direction, it is even more of a circular proposition—since here no independent and unambiguous measure exists of the size of a bundle of goods: one bundle can be identified as larger than another only if it satisfies the individual more. Indices of *per capita* income all seek to approximate the increase in individual welfare on the assumption of unchanged tastes.

The problem with applying these concepts to historical growth is that it is rarely, if ever, a simple matter of expansion along unchanged utility functions. Almost all observed growth processes have been accompanied, and most have been set off by changes in preferences. The historical transition from stagnation to growth is sometimes induced by expanding investment opportunities with tastes unchanged. More often, however, the initiating factor is a rise in material aspirations, an increased desire for goods and services generated by the example of advanced living standards elsewhere. The demonstration effect is a potent force behind most growth processes. Indeed, except where the rate of return on investment rises exogenously, it would seem to be a necessary condition for growth; for only an intensified desire for higher living standards can reconcile people to the increased present sacrifices that growth here would require.

But if taste changes are a part of the process of growth, it is no longer legitimate to interpret this process in terms of an increase in welfare. The higher consumption standards of development may yet leave people more dissatisfied than ever. Indeed, it may not be utterly implausible to argue that the evidence suggests an inverse relationship between *per capita* income and social welfare. A highly significant positive correlation exists between the ranking orders of countries by *per capita* income and by suicide rate (per thousand of population). And surely the suicide rate is the most irrefutable behavioural index of unhappiness—indicating as it does the rate of preference for death over life.

Even if we reject the extreme view foreshadowed by the evidence on suicide rates, there is the evidence of the various opinion surveys which, according to Easterlin (16), show no definite cross-sectional relationship between *per capita* income and personal happiness in different societies. Easterlin interprets this in terms of Duesenberry's hypothesis that utility is a function of relative, rather than absolute, income, and argues that the income distribution within a society rather than its average income level is the crucial determinant of individual welfare. This interpretation does not square well with the evidence of the suicide rates which, of course, are the highest of all in the socialist countries, where presumably incomes are relatively equally distributed. Nor does it take into account the curious fact disclosed by the surveys that the happiest cultures seem to be remote backward communities which have not yet been penetrated by the example of western ways of life—a fact which points to the importance of the international demonstration effect rather than the internal. Of course, accepting Easterlin's assessment of the opinion surveys does not commit us to accepting his explanation. The fact remains that development, whether regarded as a historical process or as a standard of cross-country comparisons, does not seem to be well correlated with individual welfare.

Nor does it help to abandon the utility criterion for growth in favour of the size criterion: consumption level per head or productive capacity per head cannot usually be measured independently of tastes. The Samuelsonian comparison of production (or consumption) possibility curves works only if one lies outside another throughout its length: but historical growth—while increasing productive capacity in most areas—extinguishes it in some fields, however limited.

It may, of course, be argued that changes in utility functions are not random processes. We have a common structure of underlying needs: preference patterns are developed out of this by adaptation to reality, by inhibitions imposed in the light of our knowledge of what is possible. Historical changes in utility functions consist simply of the successive withdrawal of inhibitions as our horizon of possibilities widens: more and more of the pattern of our basic needs is thus unfolded and fulfilled in the process of growth.

In a sense, this model postulates an unconscious preference pattern underlying our conscious scales of preference. Unfortunately, modern psychology does not bear out such a postulate. Our basic needs or drives do not exist in the subconscious as a rational ordering with its properties of consistency, transitivity, reflexivity, and the like. They constitute rather a bundle of unresolved conflicts. It is through interaction with the environment, through learning processes, that a semblance of order is imposed on them; and this order is almost always restricted to the plane of consciousness. Below the surface, explosive subconscious impulses simmer ready to erupt at the touch of experience in forms unintegrated with the conscious preference ordering, or even perhaps to be ultimately rationalized and integrated into a new ordering. Sufficient exposure to addictive drugs, for instance, gives rise to a behaviour pattern which has little link with pre-existing wants; if a large enough number of people are exposed, new systems of values and preferences may emerge based on the addiction and unrelated to old taste patterns. Now, an addiction will hardly be regarded as an upward step on some basic hierarchy of human needs. And general opinion presumably would not rate the drug counterculture or the spread of the opium habit in nineteenth-century China as opening up new vistas for economic development.

Yet, neither the utilitarian nor the revealed preference theorist can in principle distinguish between an addiction and a revolution of rising expectations. Both result from exposure to new consumption patterns, both induce changes in tastes or observed behaviour. A social welfare function based on individual utilities or preferences gives us no means of asserting that one points the way to growth while the other does not.

Indeed, if an addiction expresses a need for oral dependence, a demonstration effect mobilizes our aggressive urge to defend or improve our status in the social hierarchy: any growth that it touches off is in that sense a zero-sum game. From Veblen to the ethologists, the powerful instinctual sources of the demonstration effect have been thoroughly explored; and there is no indication that they are either more or less rational than those that give rise to addictions.

How then, can one distinguish between narcotic bliss and 'growth' propelled by the demonstration effect without a paternalistic decision in favour of certain instincts and against others? There is an answer to this question, of course; but it belongs to the domain of biology, not welfare economics. Processes which we intuitively recognize as growth produce improvements in various biological indices—notably life expectancy: other kinds of changes do not. Indeed, biological improvement might be described as the necessary and sufficient condition for economic growth in a closed population. Increase in welfare, on the other hand, is not only a disputable criterion but may not even be a scientifically meaningful one.

Economic growth has a variety of biological implications, of course. There is the control of epidemic diseases, the improvement in nutritional standards, the increase in height, weight, and strength of the typical individual, the acceleration of physiological maturation. But the index that best sums up the biology of growth is life expectancy.

Growth has an extensive dimension as well as this intensive one. In terms of the traditional criterion, one may think of increase in total income with *per capita* income constant as well as of *per capita* income increase. The biological counterpart of the former is population growth with constant life expectancy. It is, of course, apparent that population growth in the short run may impair life expectancy in the long (just as it erodes *per capita* incomes)— leading perhaps to an eventual arrest or reversal of the growth in numbers itself. But I am not here concerned with the distinctions between short and long-run phenomena or the conflicts between the extensive and intensive aspects of growth. These exist for the traditional income criteria as well as for the biological ones I propose. They are, therefore, irrelevant for a choice between the two.

Related to this point is the answer to the objection many biologists have to the use of proliferation in numbers as an index of evolutionary success. Overpopulation in any species culminating in Malthusian disasters like mass starvation or suicide is well known to biology and would not count as progress with biologists. The source of confusion here is that to the biologist 'progress' or 'success' has a very long-run interpretation; overpopulation on the other hand is sustainable only in the short run. Few biologists would deny that a species which, in the very long run, has maintained a significant rate of growth is an evolutionary success. Further, economists—unlike biologists—have a use for short-run measures of progress; and they should have them, recognizing all the while the potentiality of conflict between long- and short-run growth.

The use of population growth as a measure of progress in its extensive dimension is far from novel. Indeed it is a revival of ideas that date back to Rousseau and Adam Smith. The intensive measures of growth, on the other hand, have evoked interest much more recently.

It should be stressed that population data are useful as an index of extensive growth only in time series analysis. I am not suggesting that population densities give any clue to the ranking of different economies on a cross-sectional scale of economic development. Since labour is so very immobile internationally, the current population of any country is the legacy of its entire past: it does not reflect its current economic level relative to those of other economies.

If the essence of growth is increase in population or longevity, one can understand the lack of correlation with individual welfare. Wilkinson (66) suggests that the vastly higher productivity per head in many sectors of a developed economy does not constitute a net addition to welfare but an indispensable adaptation to the vastly more complex problems of urban-industrial living. Thus modern transport industries essentially cater to the higher mobility requirements of industrial life; the press and electronic media simply fill the void left by the disappearance of the close personal contacts and personalized entertainment of agrarian societies; food processing is largely a function of the distance in space and time between production and consumption in modern economies; urban construction, civic amenities, and public health facilities are the by-products of urban congestion. In other words, the essential demographic characteristics of growth necessitate a sequence of adaptations which multiply many measurable outputs manifold without necessarily adding to utility.

If one defines growth as increase in longevity or as population growth with constant life expectancy, the characteristic time-pattern of historical growth would appear very different from what it is usually assumed to be. Economic growth curves would seem to be more often logistic than exponential. They would thus accord more closely with the usual profile of biological growth.

This biological definition of growth has no normative significance whatsoever. I imply no value judgements about what growth *ought* to involve. Indeed I am remaining at the moment neutral on the ethical question of the desirability of growth. All I suggest is that biological improvement is the essence of the process that we intuitively recognize as growth—but that we do not know this and persist instead in the happy illusion that it is increase in individual welfare with which we are concerned.

While the biological definition of growth would deprive normative economists of one of their markets, it would link growth theory with the mainstream of scientific tradition. Economic growth as we know it can be generally identified as the adaptive response of the human species to its environment—an open-ended adaptation with the help of technology and culture, those tools which man alone of all animals is biologically equipped to make and use. Growth as such is an extension of organic evolution and biology lends it a direction and a rationale. Or, to put it differently, growth is a continuing search for biological survival value; and a direct measure of its success in this area is surely the best index of development.

REFERENCES

1 ARROW, K. J., 'The economic implications of learning by doing', *Review of Economic Studies* (June 1962).
2 BALDWIN, R. E., 'Patterns of development in newly settled regions', *Manchester School of Economics and Social Studies*, XXIV (May 1956).
3 BERRILL, K. E., 'International trade and the rate of economic growth', *Economic History Review*, II, XII (1960).
4 BLUM, J., *Lord and Peasant in Russia from the IXth to the XIXth Century* (London, Princeton, 1961).
5 BOSERUP, ESTHER, *The Conditions of Agricultural Growth: The Economics of Agrarian Change under Population Pressure* (Aldine, 1965).
6 BOULDING, K. E., 'Income or welfare?' *Review of Economic Studies*, V, 17, No. 2 (1949–50).
7 CARR-SAUNDERS, A. M. *The Population Problem: A Study in Human Evolution* (London, 1922).
8 DAHRENDORF, RALF, *Class and Class Conflict in Industrial Society* (London, 1976).
9 DARLINGTON, C. D., *The Evolution of Man and Society* (London, 1969).
10 DAVID, PAUL *Technical Choice, Innovation and Economic Growth* (Cambridge, 1975).
11 DAVIS, R. 'England's foreign trade, 1700–74', *Economic History Review*, II, XV (1962).
12 ——, *A Commercial Revolution* (London, 1978).
13 DEANE, P. and COLE, W. A., *British Economic Growth, 1688–1959* (Cambridge, 1962).
14 DOPSCH, ALFONS, *Economic and Social Foundation of European Civilization* (London, 1937).
15 DURAND, J. D., 'The modern expansion of world population', *Proc. Am. Phil. Soc.*, III, no. 3 (1967).
16 EASTERLIN, R. C., 'Does economic growth improve the human lot? Some empirical evidence', in P. A. David and M. W. Reder (eds.), *Nations and Households in Economic Growth: Essays in Honor of Moses Abramovitz* (New York, 1974).
17 ELVIN, MARK, *The Pattern of the Chinese Past* (London, 1973).
18 ——, 'Last thousand years of Chinese history', *Modern Asian Studies*, 4, 2, 106 (1960).
19 GERSCHENKRON, ALEXANDER, *Economic Backwardness in Historical Perspective: A Book of Essays* (Cambridge, 1966).

20 GRILICHES, Z., 'Hybrid Corn: an exploration in the economics of technological change', *Econometrica* (October 1957).
21 HABAKKUK, H. J., 'The economic history of modern Britain', *Journal of Economic History* (1958).
22 ——, 'Historical experience of economic development', in E.A.G. Robinson (ed.), *Problems in Economic Development: Proceedings of a Conference held by the International Economic Association* (London, 1965).
23 HANLEY, S. B. and YAMAMURA, K. 'Population trends and economic growth in pre-industrial Japan', in D. V. Glass and R. Revelle (eds.), *Population and Social Change* (London, 1972).
24 HARTWELL, R. M., 'The Causes of the Industrial Revolution: An essay in methodology', *Economic History Review*, II, XVII (1965).
25 HENRY, L., *Anciennes familles genévoises* (Paris, 1956).
26 HENRY, LOUIS, *Population: Analysis and Models*, Tr. by E. Van de Walle and E. F. Jones (London, 1976).
27 HICKS, J., *Theory of Economic History* (London, 1969).
28 ——, *A Contribution to the Theory of the Trade Cycle* (London, 1950).
29 HIRST, L. FABIAN, *The conquest of Plague: A Study of the Evolution of Epidemiology* (Oxford, 1953).
30 HOBBES, THOMAS, *Leviathan* (London, 1973).
31 HUNTINGTON, ELLSWORTH, *Principles of Human Geography*, 6th ed., revised by E. B. Shaw (New York, 1970).
32 KENNEDY, C., 'Induced bias in innovation and the theory of distribution', *Economic Journal* (September 1964).
33 KOESTLER, A., *The Act of Creation* (London, 1964).
34 KUZNETS, S., *Six Lectures on Economic Growth* (New York, 1959).
35 LANGER, W. L., 'Europe's initial population explosion', *American History Review* (1965).
36 LEVIN, J. V., *The Export Economies: Their Pattern of Development in Historical Perspective* (Cambridge, 1960).
37 LOMBARD, JEAN, *Mahomet et Charlemagne; le problème économique* (Annales, Économie Sociétés, Civilisations, 1948).
38 MALINOWSKI, B., *Scientific Theory of Culture and Other Essays* (Chapel Hill, 1965).
39 MANSFIELD, E., *Industrial Research and Technological Innovation: An Econometric Analysis* (London, 1969).
40 MARSHALL, ALFRED, *Principles of Economics*, 8th ed. (London, 1974).
41 MCKEOWN, THOMAS, *The Modern Rise of Population* (New York, 1976).
42 NORDHAUS, W. D., *Invention, Growth, and Welfare: A Theoretical Treatment of Technological Change* (Cambridge, Mass., 1969).
43 NURKSE, R., *Problems of Capital Formation in Underdeveloped Countries* (Oxford, 1953).

44 PARSONS, TALCOTT, *The Social System* (Illinois, 1951).
45 —— and SMELSER, N., *Economy and Society* (Glencoe, Ill., 1956).
46 PERKINS, DWIGHT, *Agricultural Development in China, 1368–1968* (Chicago, 1969).
47 —— (ed.), *China's Modern Economy in Historical Perspective* (Stanford, California, 1975).
48 PIRENNE, HENRI, *Economic and Social History of Medieval Europe* (London, 1965).
49 POPPER, KARL R., *Conjectures and Refutations: The Growth of Scientific Knowledge* (London, 1963).
50 RAZZELL, P. E., 'Population change in eighteenth-century England: A Reinterpretation', *Economic History Review*, II, XVII (1965).
51 RISKIN, CARL, 'Surplus and stagnation in modern China', in Dwight Perkins (ed.), *China's Modern Economy in Historical Perspective* (Stanford, California, 1975).
52 ROSENSTEIN-RODAN, P. N., 'Problems of industrialization of eastern and south-eastern Europe', *Economic Journal* (June–September 1943).
53 ROSTOW, W. W., *The Stages of Economic Growth: A Non-Communist Manifesto* (Cambridge, 1960).
54 SACHS, IGNACY, *Foreign Trade and Economic Development in Underdeveloped Countries* (Bombay, 1965).
55 SCHMOOKLER, J., *Invention and Economic Growth* (Cambridge, Mass., 1966).
56 SCITOVSKY, TIBOR, 'Two concepts of external economies', *Journal of Political Economy* (April 1954).
57 SMITH, THOMAS C., *The Agrarian Origins of Modern Japan* (Stanford, California, 1959).
58 ——, *Political Change and Industrial Development in Japan: Government Enterprise, 1868–1880* (Stanford, California,1955).
59 TAEUBER, I . B., *The Population of Japan* (Princeton, 1958).
60 TOYNBEE, ARNOLD J., *A Study of History* (London, 1965).
61 WEISZACKER, C. C., 'Tentative notes on a two-sector model with induced technical progress', *Review of Economic Studies* (1966).
62 WILSON, C., 'Economy and society in late Victorian Britain', *Economic History Review*, II, XVII (1965).
63 ——, 'The economic decline of the Netherlands', *Economic History Review*, I (1939).
64 ——, 'Cloth production and international competition in the 17th century', *Economic History Review*, II, XVII (1960).
65 ——, 'Taxation and the Decline of Empires', in C. Wilson, *Economic History and the Historian* (London, 1969).
66 WILKINSON, RICHARD G., *Poverty and Progress* (London, 1972).
67 WITTFOGEL, KARL A., *Oriental Despotism: A Comparative Study of*

Total Power (New Haven, 1970).

68 WRIGHT, SEWALL, *Evolution and the Genetics of Populations;* II: *The Theory of Gene Frequencies* (Chicago, 1969).

69 WRIGLEY, E. A., *Population and History* (World University Library, 1969).

70 ——, 'Family limitation in pre-industrial England', *Economic History Review*, II, XVIII (1966).

71 ——, *Industrial Growth and Population Change* (Cambridge, 1960).

SELECT BIBLIOGRAPHY

ALLEN, G. C., *A Short Economic History of Modern Japan, 1867–1937* (London, 1951).

ARDREY, R., *The Territorial Imperative* (Atheneum, New York, 1966).

——, *The Social Contract* (Atheneum, New York, 1970).

ARROW, K. J., 'The economic implications of learning by doing', *Review of Economic Studies* (June 1962).

ASHLEY MONTAGU, M. F. (ed.), *Culture and the Evolution of Man* (Oxford University Press, 1962).

ASHTON, T. S., *An Economic History of England: The 18th Century* (London, 1955).

BALDWIN, R. E., 'Patterns of development in newly settled regions', *Manchester School of Economics and Social Studies,* XXIV (May 1956).

BANTON, M. (ed.), *Darwin and the Study of Society* (Chicago, 1961).

BAYKOV, ALEXANDER, *The Development of the Soviet Economic System* (London, 1946).

BEASLEY, W. G., *The Meiji Restoration* (Stanford, California, 1972).

BERGSON, ABRAM, *The Real National Income of Soviet Russia since 1928* (Harvard, 1961).

BERKOWITZ, L., *Aggression: A Social Psychological Analysis* (New York, 1962).

BERRILL, K. E., 'International trade and the rate of economic growth', *Economic History Review,* XII, No. 3 (1960).

BLACKWELL, W. L. (ed.), *Russian Economic Development from Peter the Great to Stalin* (New York, 1974).

BLOCH, M., *Feudal Society* (London, 1961).

BLUM, J., *Lord and Peasant in Russia from the IXth to the XIXth Century* (London, Princeton, 1961).

BORTON, HUGH, *Japan's Modern Century* (New York, 1955).

BOSERUP, ESTHER, *The Conditions of Agricultural Growth: The Economics of Agrarian Change under Population Pressure* (Aldine, 1965).

BOULDING, K. E., 'Income or welfare?', *Review of Economic Studies,* V, 17, No. 2 (1949–50).

BUCK, JOHN L., *Land Utilization in China* (Shanghai, 1937).

CAIRNCROSS, A. K., *Factors in Economic Development* (London, 1965).

CAMPBELL, B. G., *Human Evolution: An Introduction to Man's Adaptations* (Aldine, Chicago, 1966).

CARR, E. H., *A History of Soviet Russia Socialism in One Country: 1924–26* (London, 1958).

——, *1917: Before and After* (London, 1969).

——, *Foundations of a Planned Economy, 1926–1929* (London, 1978).

CARR-SAUNDERS, A. M., *The Population Problem: A Study in Human Evoluton* (London, 1922).

CHI-MING HOU, *Foreign Investment and Economic Development in China, 1840–1937* (Cambridge, Mass., 1965).

CHILDE, V. G., *What Happened in History?* (Penguin, 1946; original, 1942).

CIPOLLA, CARLO M. (ed.), *Economic History of Europe*, 3 (London, 1973).

COHN, STANLEY H., 'Soviet growth retardation: Trends in resource availability and efficiency', in US Congress, Joint Economic Committee, *New Directions in the Soviet Economy* (Washington, DC, 1966).

COMFORT, A., *Nature and Human Nature* (London, 1966).

COOK, S. F., Human sacrifice and warfare as factors in the demography of pre-colonial Mexico', *Human Biology*, 18 (1946).

DAHRENDORF, RALF, *Class and Class Conflict in Industrial Society* (London, 1976).

DARLINGTON, C. D., *The Evolution of Man and Society* (London, 1969).

DARWIN, C., *The Origin of Species by Means of Natural Selection* (1859).

——, *The Descent of Man* (Murray, 1871).

DAVID, PAUL, *Technical Choice, Innovation and Economic Growth* (Cambridge, 1975).

DAVIS, R., 'England's foreign trade, 1700–74', *Economic History Review*, II, XV, 1962.

——, *A Commercial Revolution* (London, 1978).

DE BEER, G., 'Evolution by natural selection', in M. Freed (ed.), *Readings in Anthropology* 1 (New York, 1968).

DEANE, P. and COLE, W. A., *British Economic Growth 1688–1959* (Cambridge, 1962).

DOBB, MAURICE, *Soviet Economic Development since 1917*, 2nd ed. (London, 1966).

DOBB, M., *Studies in the Development of Capitalism* (London, 1963).

DONNITHORNE, AUDREY G., *China's Economic System* (London, 1967).

DOPSCH, ALFONS, *Economic and Social Foundation of European Civilization* (London, 1937).

DOUGLAS, M., Population control in primitive groups', *British Journal of Sociology* (1966).

DUBOS, R., *So Human an Animal* (New York, 1968).

DUBY, G., *Early Growth of the European Economy: Warriors and Peasants from the Seventh to the Twelfth Century* (New York, 1974).

DUESENBERRY, J. S., *Income, Saving and the Theory of Consumer Behaviour* (Cambridge, 1969).

DURAND, J. D., 'The modern expansion of world population', *Proc. Am. Phil. Soc.*, III, no. 3 (1967).

EASTERLIN, R. C., 'Does economic growth improve the human lot? Some empirical evidence', in P. A. David and M. W. Reder (eds.), *Nations and Households in Economic Growth: Essays in Honor of Moses Abramovitz* (New York, 1974).

ECKSTEIN, ALEXANDER, GALENSON, WALTER, and TA-CHUNG LIU (eds.), *Economic Trends in Communist China* (Chicago, 1968).

ELVIN, MARK, *The Pattern of the Chinese Past* (London, 1973).

——, 'The Last Thousand Years of Chinese History', *Modern Asian Studies*, 4, 2, 106 (1960).

ENGELS, F., *Origins of the Family, Private Property, and the State* (Chicago, 1905).

ERLICH, ALEXANDER, *The Soviet Industrialization Debates 1924–1928* (Harvard, 1960).

FAIRBANK, JOHN K., ECKSTEIN, ALEXANDER, and YANG, L. S., 'Economic change in early modern China: An analytic framework', *Economic Development and Cultural Change*, 9–10 (3–4 October 1960).

FEUERWERKER, ALBERT, *China's Early Industrialization* (Cambridge, Mass., 1958).

——, *The Chinese Economy, 1912–1949* (Ann Arbor, Mich., 1968).

FINLEY, M. I., *The Ancient Economy* (London, 1973).

FITZGERALD, C. P., *Birth of Communist China* (Penguin, 1970).

GALBRAITH, J. K., *The Affluent Society* (London, 1960).

GARN S. M. (ed.), *Culture and the Direction of Human Evolution* (Wayne State University, Detroit, Mich., 1964)

GERSCHENKRON, ALEXANDER, *Economic Backwardness in Historical Perspective: A Book of Essays* (Cambridge, 1966).

GOLDSMITH, RAYMOND, 'The economic growth of Tsarist Russia 1860–1913', *Economic Development and Cultural Change*, IX (1961).

GOODRICH, L. C., *A Short History of the Chinese People* (London, 1962).

GRILICHES, Z., Hybrid corn: an exploration in the economics of technological change', *Econometrica* (October 1957).

HABAKKUK, H. J., 'The economic history of Modern Britain', *Journal of Economic History* (1958).

——, 'Historical experience of economic development', in E.A.G. Robinson (ed.), *Problems in Economic Development: Proceedings of a Conference held by the International Economic Association* (London, 1965).

HANLEY, S. B., and YAMAMURA, K., 'Population trends and economic growth in pre-industrial Japan', in D. V. Glass and R. Revelle (eds.), *Population and Social Change* (London, 1972).

HARTWELL, R. M., 'The causes of the Industrial Revolution: An essay in methodology', *Economic History Review*, II, XVII (1965).

HENRY, L., *Anciennes familles génévoises* (Paris, 1956).

HENRY, LOUIS, *Population: Analysis and Models*, tr. by E. Van de Walle and E. F. Jones (London, 1976).

HICKS, J., *Theory of Economic History* (London, 1969).

——, *A Contribution to the Theory of the Trade Cycle* (London, 1950).

HIRSCHMEIER, JOHANNES, *The Origins of Entrepreneurship in Meiji Japan* (Cambridge, Mass., 1964).

HIRST, L. FABIAN, *The Conquest of Plague; A Study of the Evolution of Epidemiology* (Oxford, 1953).

HOBBES, THOMAS, *Leviathan* (London, 1973).

HOBSBAWM, E. J. and HARTWELL, R. M., 'The standard of living during the Industrial Revolution: A discussion', *Economic History Review*, II, XVI (1963).

——, *Industry and Empire: An Economic History of Britain since 1750* (London, 1969).

HOPKINS, K.,'Economic growth and towns in classical antiquity', in P. Abrams and E. A. Wrigley (eds.), *Towns in Societies* (Cambridge, 1978).

HUNTINGTON, ELLSWORTH, *Principles of Human Geography*, 6th ed. revised by E. B. Shaw (New York, 1970).

HUXLEY, J. S., *Evolution: The Modern Synthesis*, 2nd ed. (Allen Unwin, 1963).

IMLAH, A. H., *Economic Elements in the Pax Britannica: Studies in British Foreign Trade in the Nineteenth Century* (New York, 1969).

JASNY, NAUM, *Soviet Industrialization 1928–1952* (Chicago, 1961).

JONES, A. H. M., *The Athenian Democracy* (Oxford, 1957).

——, *The Later Roman Empire* (Oxford, 1969).

——, and BRUNT, P. A. (eds.), *Roman Economy: Studies in Ancient Economic and Administrative History* (Oxford, 1974).

——, 'The Economic Basis of Athenian Democracy', *Past and Present*, no.1 (1952).

KANG CHAO, *Agricultural Production in Communist China, 1949–1965* (Madison, Wis., 1970).

KENNEDY, C., 'Induced bias in innovation and the theory of distribution', *Economic Journal* (September 1964).

KOESTLER, A., *The Act of Creation* (London, 1964).

KUNG-CHUAN HSIAO, *Rural China: Imperial Control in the Nineteenth Century* (Seattle, 1960).

KUZNETS, S., *Six Lectures on Economic Growth* (New York, 1959).

LACK, D., *The Natural Regulation of Animal Numbers* (Oxford, 1954).

LANDES, D., *Unbound Prometheus: Technological Change and Industrial Development in Western Europe from 1750 to the Present* (London, 1970).

LANGER, W. L., 'Europe's initial population explosion', *American History Review* (1965).

LATOUCHE, R., *The Birth of the Western Economy* (New York, 1961).

LEVIN, J. V., *The Export Economies: Their Pattern of Development in Historical Perspective* (Cambridge, 1960).

LIU, T. C. and YEH, K. C., *The Economy of the Chinese Mainland* (Princeton, 1965).

LOCKWOOD, W.W., *The Economic Development of Japan* (London, 1955).

LOMBARD, JEAN, *Mahomet et Charlemagne: le Problème Économique* (Annales, Économie, Sociétés, Civilisations, 1948).

LORENZ, K., *King Solomon's Ring* (London, 1952).

——, *On Aggression* (London, 1966).

MALINOWSKI, B., *A Scientific Theory of Culture and Other Essays* (Chapel Hill, 1965).

MANSFIELD, E., *Industrial Research and Technological Innovation: An Econometric Analysis* (London, 1969).

MAO TSE-TUNG, *Selected Works of Mao Tse-Tung* (Peking, 1965).

MARSHALL, ALFRED, *Principles of Economics*, 8th ed. (London, 1974).

MARX, K. and ENGELS, F., *Communist Manifesto, Socialist Landmark*, Original text plus a new appreciation written for the Labour Party by H. J. Laski (London, 1948, Orig. 1888)

MARX, K., *Writings of the Young Marx on Philosophy and Society*, L. D. Easton and K. H. Guddat (eds.)(New York, 1967).

——, *Capital: A Critical Analysis of Capitalist Production*, 3rd German ed., tr. by S. Moore and E. Aveling (ed.), S. Sonnenschein (Lowrey and Co., London, 1887).

MATHIAS, PETER, *First Industrial Nation: Economic History of Britain, 1700–1914* (London, 1969).

MCKEOWN, THOMAS, *The Modern Rise of Population* (New York, 1976).

MONTAGU, A. (ed.), *Culture and the Evolution of Man* (Oxford University Press, 1962).

MOORE, BARRINGTON, *Social Origins of Dictatorship and Democracy* (Boston, 1967).

MORRIS, D., *The Naked Ape* (London, 1972).

——, *The Human Zoo* (New York, 1970).

MUMFORD, L. *Technics and Civilization* (New York, 1934).

MYERS, RAMON H., *The Chinese Peasant Economy* (Cambridge, Mass., 1970).

NEEDHAM, JOSEPH, *Science and Civilisation in China* (Cambridge, 1965).

NORDHAUS, W. D., *Invention, Growth, and Welfare: A Theoretical Treatment of Technological Change* (Cambridge, Mass., 1969).

NORMAN, E. H., *Japan's Emergence as a Modern State* (New York, Institute of Pacific Relations, 1940).

NOVE, ALEC, *An Economic History of the U. S. S. R.* (London, 1969).

——, *The Soviet Economy: An Introduction* (London, 1968).

NURKSE, R., *Problems of Capital Formation in Underdeveloped Countries* (Oxford, 1953).

PARSONS, TALCOTT, *The Social System* (Illinois, 1951).

——, and SMELSER, N., *Economy and Society* (Glencoe, Ill., 1956).

PERKINS, DWIGHT, *Agricultural Development in China, 1368–1968* (Chicago, 1969).

——, (ed.), *China's Modern Economy in Historical Perspective* (Stanford, California, 1975).

PING-TI HO, *The Ladder of Success in Imperial China* (New York, 1962).

PIRENNE, HENRI, *Economic and Social History of Medieval Europe* (London, 1965).

POLANYI, K., *et al.*, *Trade and Markets in Early Empires* (Glencoe, Ill., 1957).

POPPER, KARL R., *Conjectures and Refutations: The Growth of Scientific Knowledge* (London, 1963).

PRYBYLA, JAN S., *The Political Economy of Communist China* (Scranton, Pa., 1970).

RAZZELL, P. E., 'Population change in eighteenth-century England: A reinterpretation', *Economic History Review*, II, XVII (1965).

REISCHAUER, EDWIN O. and FAIRBANK J. K. *A History of East Asian Civilization;* I, *East Asia: The Great Tradition* (Boston, 1960); II, *East Asia: The Modern Transformation* (Boston, 1964).

RISKIN, CARL, 'Surplus and stagnation in modern China', in Dwight Perkins (ed.), *China's Modern Economy in Historical Perspective* (Stanford, California, 1975).

ROSENSTEIN-RODAN, P. N., 'Problems of industrialization of eastern and south-eastern Europe', *Economic Journal* (June–September 1943).

ROSTOVZEFF, M., *Social and Economic History of the Roman Empire*, 2nd ed. (Oxford, 1957).

ROSTOW, W. W., *The Stages of Economic Growth, A Non-Communist Manifesto* (Cambridge, 1960).

RUSSELL, W. M. S. and RUSSELL, C., *Human Behaviour* (London, 1961).

SACHS, IGNACY, *Foreign Trade and Economic Development in Underdeveloped Countries* (Bombay, 1965).

SANSOM, GEORGE, *A History of Japan*, I (London, 1958).

——, *The Western World and Japan* (London, 1950).

SCHMOOKLER, J., *Invention and Economic Growth* (Cambridge, Mass., 1966).

SCHWARTZ, HARRY, *The Soviet Economy since Stalin* (New York, 1965).

SCITOVSKY, TIBOR, 'Two concepts of external economies', *Journal of Political Economy* (April 1954).

SIMPSON, G. G., *The Meaning of Evolution* (New Haven, 1950).

——, 'The biological nature of man', *Science*, 152 (1966).

SMITH, THOMAS C., *The Agrarian Origins of Modern Japan* (Stanford, California, 1959).

——, *Political Change and Industrial Development in Japan: Government Enterprise, 1868–1880* (Stanford, California, 1955).

SNOW, EDGAR, *Red Star Over China* (New York, 1961).

SOUTHERN, R. W., *The Making of the Middle Ages* (London, 1959).

SPUHLER, J. N. (ed.), *The Evolution of Man's Capacity for Culture* (Wayne State University Press, Detroit, Mich., 1959).

STORR, A., *Human Aggression* (London, 1968).

TAEUBER, I. B., *The Population of Japan* (Princeton, 1958).

THOMPSON, L., 'A self-regulating system of human population control', *Proc. N. Y. Academy of Sciences* (1970).

TINBERGEN, N., *The Study of Instinct* (Oxford, 1951).

——, *Social Behaviour in Animals* (New York, 1953).

TOYNBEE, ARNOLD J., *A Study of History* (London, 1965).

VEBLEN, THORSTEIN, *The Theory of the Leisure Class: An Economic Study of Institutions* (London, 1924).

VON LAUE, THEODORE, *Sergei Witte and the Industrialization of Russia* (New York, 1963).

WASHBURN, S. L., 'Speculations on the inter-relations of the history of tools and biological evolution' in J. N. Spuhler (ed.), *The Evolution of Man's Capacity for Culture* (Wayne State University Press, Detroit, Mich., 1959).

WEISZACKER C. C., 'Tentative notes on a two-sector model with induced technical progress', *Review of Economic Studies* (1966).

WILSON, C., 'Economy and society in late Victorian Britain', *Economic History Review*, II, XVII (1965).

——, 'The economic decline of the Netherlands', *Economic History Review*, I (1939).

——, 'Cloth production and international competition in the 17th century', *Economic History Review*, II (1960).

——, 'Taxation and the decline of Empires', in C. Wilson, *Economic History and the Historian* (London, 1969).

WILKINSON, RICHARD G., *Poverty and Progress* (London, 1972).

WITTFOGEL, KARL A., *Oriental Despotism: A Comparative Study of Total Power* (New Haven, 1970).

WRIGHT, J. F., 'British economic growth 1688–1959', *Economic History Review*, II, XVII (1965).

WRIGHT, SEWALL, *Evolution and the Genetics of Populations*; II, *The Theory of Gene Frequencies* (Chicago, 1969).

WRIGLEY, E. A., *Population and History* (World University Library, 1969).

——, 'Family limitation in pre-industrial England', *Economic History Review* (1966).

——, *Industrial Growth and Population Change* (Cambridge, 1960).